I0727987

Franz Grabmayr

Opera 1970–1980

Paintings from the Vienna State Opera

with a text by
Robert Fleck

edited by
Jakob Grabmayr / Grabmayr Estate

Snoeck

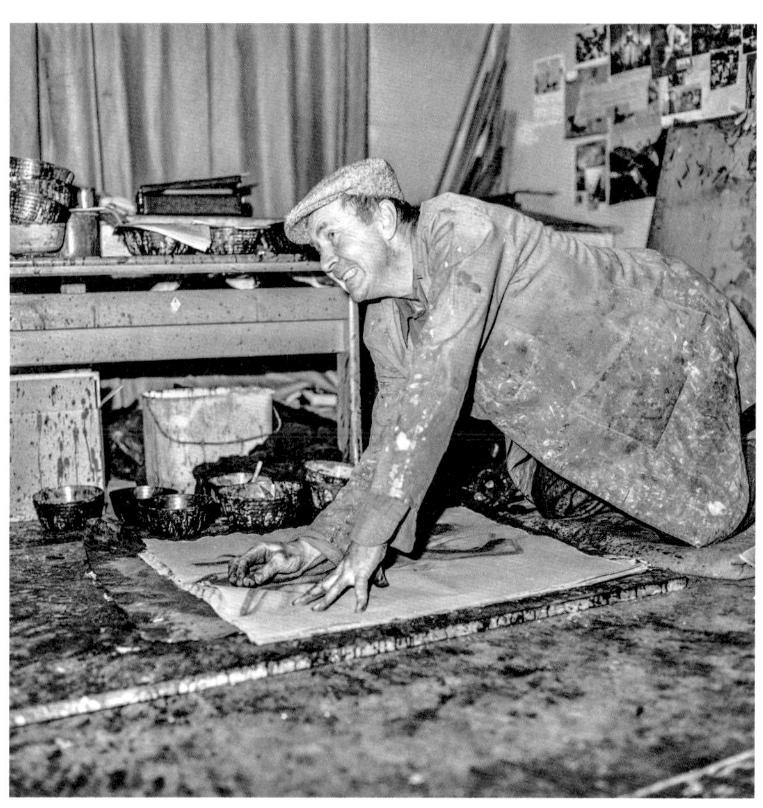

Robert Fleck
Franz Grabmayr paints

Franz Grabmayr paints. He doesn't paint just anywhere, he paints at the Vienna State Opera. He doesn't paint just anywhere inside the Vienna State Opera, but onstage. And not just any old time, but in the evenings during ballet performances. He paints the movements of the dancers of the Vienna State Opera Ballet, observing them in situ. He is concealed to the right of the auditorium between one of the three side curtains. Most of the time, he just watches with the utmost concentration. Then he paints, very swiftly, with colored and black inks on paper, never taking his eyes off the moving bodies. The paintings on paper, exhibited and published here for the first time, were created "blindly", without the painter ever looking at them as he executed them. His gaze would never leave the movements of the dancers on stage at the State Opera, even during the short moment when he moved the freshly painted sheet to the side in order to immediately have a new sheet ready from a thick pile of drawing paper he had brought with him.

The works from the Vienna State Opera that Franz Grabmayr created in the winter months between 1970 and 1980 derive their fervency

from this particular constellation.[1] These are
not paintings of the ballet as a whole, nor of
the individual dancers. You won't find dancers
in pairs or groups, as they regularly appear
in ballet. Movement as such, or rather individual dance steps and body constellations within
the space on stage, are captured in abbrevi-
ated forms, reduced to their innermost essence.
One senses that this has been seen and painted
"live", perceived directly in the ballet, and
executed on the thick watercolor paper without
any intermediate steps. Movement – concrete,
extremely artistic and professional movement –
is captured in pictures that break new ground
in their concatenation of abstraction and
figuration. Movement in this instance derives
from painting. This is quite unlike any pre-
vious attempts of mechanical reproduction of
movement in the visual arts. Moreover, Franz
Grabmayr developed a new vocabulary and a new
notion of the image while painting in view of
the ballet of the Vienna State Opera. This
vocabulary has guided his work ever since, and
its great significance is gradually being
recognized today.[2] Grabmayr's paintings on
paper, executed at the Vienna State Opera,
are shown here for the first time. We chart a
selection of twenty-nine sheets from the years
1970 to 1980, put together by the artist still
during his lifetime, that was recently discovered in his estate.

Franz Grabmayr was forty-three years old when he began his work with the ballet at the Vienna State Opera. It had only been six years since he had completed his studies at the Academy of Fine Arts in Vienna. As a child of a mountain farmer, he initially became a secondary school teacher in Carinthia. It was only relatively late in life that he had the opportunity to study art and become an artist.[3] In the 1970s, only a few fellow artists were familiar with his work. After finishing his studies, he painted from spring to fall in isolation in the northern Waldviertel, a region northwest of Vienna that was then quite remote, not far from the Czechoslovakian border, in other words very close to the Iron Curtain at the time. The northern Waldviertel is furthermore considered to be the coldest region in Austria. It did however offer him the opportunity to spend the whole day observing a landscape that had not yet been industrialized, and to paint in direct confrontation with it. He would then stay in Vienna for the winter months in a one-room studio in Favoritenstrasse, painting continually and spending just one or two days at weekends with his family in Vienna's sixteenth district.[4] His first solo exhibition, which attracted some attention, took place in 1973 at the Vienna Secession, yet it remained largely inconsequential.

Who was it that gave this then unknown artist permission to be present at the rehearsals of the State Opera Ballet and later also on stage during performances, all the while working freely, without any constraints or control? According to the recollections of the State Opera dancers during those years, he was suddenly there, initially drawing in the ballet hall. Someone had given him permission. He was never introduced to them. But someone must have authorized it, otherwise he wouldn't have suddenly been there.

This was rather typical of Vienna around 1970, one might say, when everything still happened in small circles and was often very informal. At a distance of forty kilometers, Vienna was surrounded by the Iron Curtain in three directions. The city, rich in tradition, was located literally at the end of the Free World. There were few encounters with foreigners. International organizations such as the UN, the Atomic Energy Agency, and the Organization of the Petroleum Exporting Countries (OPEC) only settled in the Austrian capital in the mid-1970s. Tourism played no role at all. The rediscovery of Viennese Modernism around 1900 only began ten years later. Both in Austria and internationally, Klimt and Schiele were merely regarded as marginal artists of no great significance. The free practice of psychoanalysis, which Sigmund Freud had founded in Vienna, remained prohibited by a National Socialist law that post-war democratic Austria initially did not revise, and was indeed never mentioned in school lessons.

All the greater was the symbolic role of the Vienna State Opera. Its reconstruction after extensive damage by bombing during the war and its ceremonial reopening on November 5, 1955, was the highest-profile cultural event of the post-war decades. The State Opera henceforth embodied Austria's viability. The reopening took place six months after the signing of the Austrian State Treaty, with which the Allied Powers, including the Soviet Union and the Red Army, had unexpectedly promised their peaceful withdrawal in return for Austria's declaration of neutrality. The reopening of the State Opera nevertheless occurred under the occupation of the four victorious powers of World War II, which only ended in the fall of 1956. The un-paralleled symbolic role of the State Opera in the Austrian post-war decades is also reflected in the lasting reverberations and trauma of the murder of a ballet girl in March 1963, when a ballet student was raped and brutally murdered in a corridor of the Vienna State Opera. Ever since this biggest criminal case of the 1960s in Austria, security at the State Opera has been a matter of national interest.

So, in the wake of such a situation, who did grant Franz Grabmayr permission to draw and paint completely freely during practice, rehearsals, and later also during the performances of the State Opera Ballet? The beginning of the artist's creative work at the Vienna State Opera falls into the period of Heinrich Reif-Gintl's directorship from 1968 to 1972, who was succeeded by Rudolf Gamsjäger from 1972 to 1976. Egon Sehfehler was State Opera director from 1976 to 1982 and then again from 1984 to 1986. He had already been deputy director of the Vienna State Opera from 1954 to 1961, that is, around the time of its reopening in 1955, before becoming deputy general director of the Deutsche Oper in Berlin from 1970. He belonged to the leading cultural circles of the Austrian People's Party, which shared the spheres of influence with the Austrian Social Democratic Party in what was then known as the Proporz. Grabmayr had been held in high esteem as an artist since his student years in Vienna, and in fact to this day, by the influential members of the Socialist Student Association. The long-standing finance minister Hannes Androsch regularly bought paintings privately and thus de facto financed the artist's studio lease. As former federal president, Heinz Fischer officially opened Grabmayr's first posthumous retrospective exhibition in February 2017 at the Museum Angerlehner in Talheim near Wels[5] with a deeply moving address.

The relationship with the VSSTÖ (Socialist Students of Austria) may well have been helpful. Ingrid Grabmayr remembers that her husband was looking for dance models for the winter months in Vienna and had met two students from the Schönbrunn Ballet School, where he wanted to work during rehearsals, which however he was not permitted to do. He then inquired at the directorate of the Vienna State Opera. A friendly older gentleman, a deputy or technical director, thought it was interesting and paved his way to work in the ballet hall, and later also at the performances. He remained his protective hand in the Vienna State Opera, making this project possible. Another source that may have facilitated his access to the State Opera was the artists' association Wiener Secession, where he was active and respected around 1970. The studio in Karl-Marx-Hof, which has been preserved to this day, was rented by the artist from the municipality of Vienna in the late 1970s. Two young artists thought it was too big and informed him that the space was empty. In order to obtain a rental contract in the Karl-Marx-Hof, the symbolic center of Red Vienna in the 1920s, which is still in existence today, connections in the VSSTÖ would at least do no harm, as the Viennese say. Things would often happen rather quickly through 'unbureaucratic' channels.[6]

For at least ten years, from 1970 to 1980, possibly a little longer, Franz Grabmayr was able to observe the ballet of the Vienna State Opera and paint freely during rehearsals and performances. "Don't trip over Grabmayr when exiting the stage," was the instruction for the dancers. Grabmayr's painting in view of the ballet dancers was a purely private learning process, as these paintings on paper were not painted for exhibition purposes.

More recent eyewitness accounts reveal that Grabmayr was received with astonishment but in a positive way by the ballet dancers, who had never before seen a visual artist paint during their practice and rehearsals. They emphasize how modest and considerate he was. Someone who doesn't belong but whom you got used to and who was part of the winter months for years before he was suddenly no longer there.

"There's someone here now, who's drawing us during exercises." Exercises, a daily occurrence lasting for hours, are the most intimate part of a ballet dancer's life. They are occupied all year round with achieving maximum control of their bodies – they are on a diet – and this sometimes for over forty years. To be able to keep up their level of performance, they work non-stop on movements that no one else could perform and – what is so unique about ballet – that they have to execute with absolute aesthetic precision, whether as part of a choreography in a group, or solo – slacking off means being left out. And this is not a sporting competition, but a three-dimensional work of art of movement that must be created as a joint effort and where everything has to be just right.

Franz Grabmayr's works from the State Opera do indeed breathe this, even though – or perhaps because – he executed them as fine art in their own right, not on commission or as part of a carefully formulated art project. At the same time, in ballet everything must have the immediacy of a first performance. Every leap, however practiced and rehearsed it may be, is the first. Otherwise, the magic of the ballet performance will not happen.

This is what the dancers work toward. Hence, they never lose their focus, even during the exercises and their executions. That, too, is evident in Grabmayr's work. The dancers moreover report that Franz Grabmayr's presence never broke their concentration, which surprised them, given that there was suddenly a painter in the ballet room, whom they in turn put into a rather distinct state of concentration. This dialectic is the secret of these sheets. Ballet training requires extreme levels of focus on the body, its gestures, the movements of the limbs and the rhythm of these movements. Translated into a representation on the surface, Franz Grabmayr's sheets from the opera immediately take us back to painting. On several of the sheets, the dancers would recognize very precise dance steps, which are part of the European ballet tradition, and which the artist captured with great precision in the spontaneity of his lines.

An infinite number of sheets were created while they were dancing right in front of him. "Sometimes he was there six days a week during the winter months." He knelt in the ballet hall and on stage, watching and painting. He was often physically very close to the dancers in the ballet hall. Rudolf Nureyev, the most famous dancer of the 1970s and 1980s, also danced for him. Grabmayr did not subsequently label the sheets with the names of the dancers, because it was about the movement, rather than the people. These kinds of processes do not take place without friction and incidents. After a solo performance on the main stage of the Vienna State Opera, Nureyev is said to have complained that Grabmayr's white sheets on the side of the stage had irritated him. This is quite understandable, after all, what is a painter who only paints for himself doing on an opera stage? Franz Grabmayr painted the movement and nothing else. He never took his eyes off the dancers, they report, looking at them intensely for long periods of time before he drew on the paper or started painting: "It was never unpleasant, because he wasn't observ-

ing us as women. He was interested in the movement," one of them explains.

Painting movement is an ancient challenge
within painting. Already in the cave paintings
of Lascaux, created some 20,000 years ago, it
is present in the distortion and deformation
of the buffaloes depicted at full gallop in
the hunting scenes. Grabmayr's works on paper
from the Vienna State Opera also breathe an
archaic quality, although he never archaizes
in the sense of imitating these origins of
painting. The cave paintings were first discovered between 1930 and 1940 and depicted in
the first encyclopedic illustrated books on
art history from the 1950s onwards. This was a

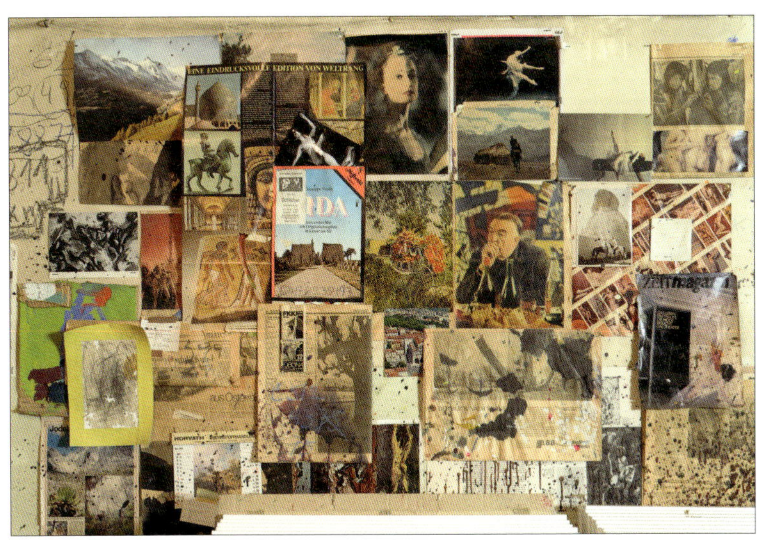

formative experience for Grabmayr's generation
and came as something of a shock. We are in
the age of the "imaginary museum", as the
writer and minister of cultural affairs André
Malraux in 1947 called the circumstance that
printed photographic reproductions now made
the entire history of art available to artists
at all times. As the reference pictures pinned
to the doors and walls of his Vienna studio
indicate, Franz Grabmayr knew European and
non-European art history very well, probably
better than most other Austrian artists of his
generation. This is also evidenced by his li-
braries in his studios in the Waldviertel and
in Vienna, as well as by the fact that during
the winter months he spent in Vienna, he vis-
ited the Kunsthistorisches Museum around fifty
times per season. He studied individual paintings in such detail that he was eventually
able to describe them by heart one square cen-
timeter at a time. He also went on (family)
trips just to see old masters.

Grabmayr's exploration of movement in painting has something original about it, something
that had never before been done. This is particularly true in the sheets from the Vienna
State Opera. Here, he developed his pictorial
vocabulary over the years, which he then continually expanded, extended and radicalized
with the *Tanzblätter* in his Vienna studio during the winter months from the 1980s onwards.

Movement in the visual arts is one of the major themes of modernism in the twentieth century, parallel to the emergence of film, automobiles, airplanes, and television. From 1910, the Italian Futurists pursued the representation of movement in a programmatic way. *Machine Art* was the title of a famous exhibition at the Museum of Modern Art in New York in 1934; *The machine as seen by the end of the mechanical age* was another legendary exhibition at the same venue in 1968, organized by Pontus Hulten. However, the works that Grabmayr created for the State Opera Ballet have virtually nothing to do with the pictorial solutions for movement in the visual arts that triumphed in the contemporary art world in the 1960s and 1970s, such as kinetics, body art, and early video and performance art.

Movement specifically is painted here as directly as possible. In the beginning, when he discovered the universe of ballet exercises, rehearsals and performances, which is generally off limits to visual artists, and developed his own working method, he still reproduced movement by drawing recognizable bodies. Later, when he was given access to the State Opera stage during ballet performances and rehearsals and began using colors, hardly any actual depictions of bodies are discernible, although it is immediately apparent that he painted in the face of ballet bodies in motion.

Those members of the State Opera Ballet at the time who we were able to track down also recall their astonishment when, after rehearsals, they were shown some sheets that had just been created by this painter, who always remained a very nice but mysterious presence as a visual artist. "I told him I knew nothing about it. He explained it to me, gave me art lessons, so to speak. Those were great moments," one of the dancers remembers.

The artistic innovation in the paintings on paper from the Vienna State Opera lies in the fact that Franz Grabmayr has developed his own pictorial language for movement, which, using abstract means of color and without expressionist distortion, places the viewer in a direct confrontation with a moving body, in a way that had never been seen before. To a certain extent, abstract means are used to reassemble moving bodies so that nothing remains of them but movement. This movement is not reproduced, but rather becomes in its inner grammar the basis of a painterly image that draws its momentum and power from the fact that it was created in the immediate vicinity of the dancers. With this ten-year work at the Vienna State Opera, which was not visible to the public, the artist created for himself a level of painting of such magnitude that it made him extremely interesting for subsequent generations, especially in the wake of Expressionism.

A clue to the chronology of these works on paper emerged in conversations with the dancers, who are contemporary witnesses of Grabmayr's work at the Vienna State Opera. The sheets with pencil and charcoal on paper must have been created in the rehearsal halls. Their floors had to be immaculately even and clean, as they would have been in any highly professional ballet hall. He would never have been allowed to paint with colored paints here, which was however possible hidden at the side of the stage. This allows us to reconstruct the development of this work at the State Opera.

Before his death in 2015, the artist compiled a meticulous selection of twenty-nine works from the countless drawings and paintings he created at the Vienna State Opera, which he labeled "Opera 1970–1980". Most of the sheets in this selection are colorful paintings on heavy artist's paper. Only a few are marked with dates. If one considers the fact that he was initially only able to work with pencil and charcoal in the rehearsal and practice halls of the State Opera Ballet before he was given permission to paint using colors hidden in the side curtains on the State Opera stage, it becomes possible to surmise how these works evolved.

It begins with charcoal drawings that are already virtuoso, consisting of only a few

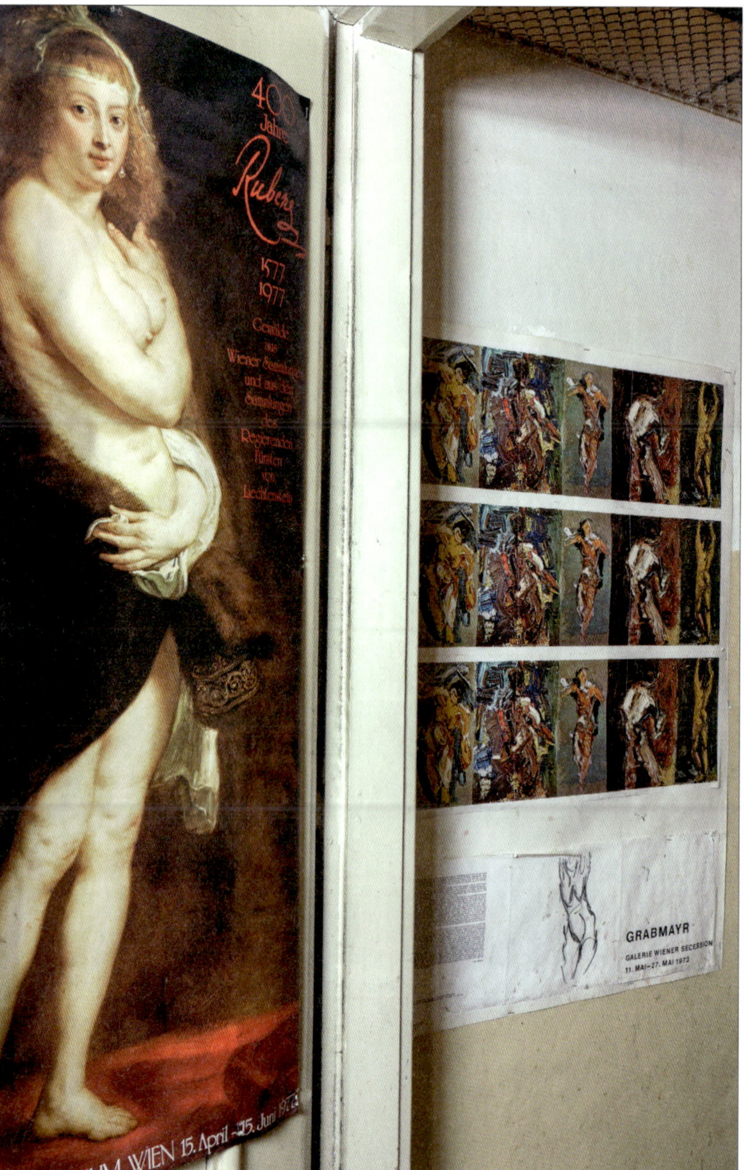
40 Jahre
Rubens
1577
1977
Gemälde
aus
Wiener Sammlungen
und aus den
Sammlungen
des
Regierenden
Fürsten
von
Liechtenstein
KUNSTHISTORISCHES MUSEUM WIEN 15. April – 15. Juni 1977
GRABMAYR
GALERIE WIENER SECESSION
11. MAI – 27. MAI 1972

lines, albeit still with recognizable torso and limbs. These probably date from the early 1970s, when the artist was in close contact with the association of artists Vienna Secession. At the time, the Secession around its president Georg Eisler was searching for renewed forms of realism, in opposition to the main currents of Western contemporary art of the time such as Op Art, Kinetic Art, Minimal Art, Conceptual Art, Happening, and Action Art.

This search for this renewed form of realism is also evident in what are probably the oldest of the works in color, which represent a figurative depiction of scenes. These include in particular the equestrian scenes, of which there are five in Grabmayr's selection. The fact that the artist included so many sheets of this type in his selection indicates the importance he attached to this theme. The State Opera at this time did indeed still own a horse and ponies, which were used in performances on stage before animal rights activists successfully campaigned to end this. Only the ponies were actually mounted in the ballet performances. Grabmayr's sheets with horse and ponies in the Vienna State Opera thus also constitute historical testimony; they exhibit great delicacy in their coloration, which may explain why the artist rated them so highly.

From around 1973, the ever greater independence of coloration and the increasing autonomization of form led Grabmayr beyond his initial realistic formal tendencies into an artistic universe that belonged to him alone. The result is a spontaneous painting in which the color scheme at first remains oriented towards the local colors of the dancing body and the color effects in the backlighting of the stage spotlights – which creates fantastic chromatic combinations – before he moves on to seemingly completely freely painted sheets in which the centrality of the human figure explodes and the color scheme once again emancipates itself, while the dynamic and the power made visible is still that of an actually dancing body.

The artist follows a similar path in his paintings on canvas produced during the warmer months of the year in the Waldviertel. Here he develops from reproducing what he sees toward a free approach with the form of "landscape paintings", in which nature remains both stimulus and corrective. These Waldviertel paintings from the late 1970s and around 1980 turned Franz Grabmayr into a paragon of the new generation of painters in Austria, and in particular of Herbert Brandl and Gunter Damisch. Around that same time, he became an international insider tip among painters such as Frank Auerbach and Leon Kossoff in London, the circle around Francis Bacon. The artist's secluded lifestyle in the Waldviertel and in his winter studio at Karl-Marx-Hof in Vienna meant that throughout his life he was unable to build on this emerging fame among fellow artists to achieve broad international recognition.

This same astonishing independence is evident in Grabmayr's selection from the Vienna State Opera, with the occasional addition of an element of great humor. There are several highly amusing duos. On one occasion, the same dancer appears to be painted completely freely in full-body profile and then, literally a moment later, translated as a swirling movement that traces a vertical screw into the space. These are magnificent paintings that make you wonder why the artist never exhibited them throughout his life, even though he was perfectly aware of the value of this work.

Grabmayr's selection of works in the portfolio *Opera 1970–1980* ends with four white sheets in black ink that display a stunning dynamism. They are simplified to the extreme and, with their stick figure form, prove to be the perfect conclusion that the artist had wrested from the ballet movements in the course of his work at the State Opera. He had mastered the métier by heart, and this is where his painterly talent is truly liberated. This was obviously easier to accomplish with

the State Opera Ballet than with the landscape
in the Waldviertel. These sheets have something of the impertinence of the "return of
painting" around 1980, which Franz Grabmayr
accompanied from a distinctly older generation, in the combination of a free painterly
approach with what he had extensively observed
and studied at the ballet.

During the final years of his work with the
State Opera Ballet, Grabmayr developed those
bundles of shapes that subsequently reappeared
in his landscape paintings, which he realized
in the Waldviertel, namely in his fire paintings. Around the same time, the plane trees
along the country roads in the Waldviertel
were felled following numerous fatal car acci-
dents. Their rootstocks were of no commercial
value. Grabmayr procured them almost free of
charge and used them to light tall fires in a
sand pit, which blazed for hours and which he
then extinguished with water he carried with
him. He would often paint these fires, seven
to eight meters in height, in the middle of
the night. From 1981 on, he would have himself
chauffeured around the fire on the trailer of
a tractor at a speed of 5 km per hour while he
observed and then spontaneously painted it.
This is where we again find the constellation
of movement, observation, and spontaneous act
of painting that he had developed in his work
with the State Opera Ballet. The fire in the

sand pit effectively took the place of the dancers.

When Franz Grabmayr painted at the Vienna State Opera, during practice, rehearsals, and performances of the State Opera Ballet, he observed and painted nothing other than movement. But it was not just any movement. At the State Opera Ballet he saw, drew, and painted movements that were conceived, developed, practiced, and executed as absolute movements. These were movements that in their precision and expressiveness went beyond anything previously known. The Vienna State Opera Ballet defines itself per se as a world-class ballet company, comparable only to very few other houses. This also means daily work at the highest level, which the artist was able to observe and translate into pictures that he would in fact paint only for himself.

In other words, he did not paint just any dancers, but instead was confronted with the very highest level of dance. Anyone who is involved with top athletes knows that their movements have nothing in common with those of even well-trained amateur athletes. You see movements of incredible efficiency and beauty that extend through the entire body. The work of the State Opera Ballet, like that of the State Opera Orchestra of the Vienna Philharmonic, consists of perfecting the movements and their sequences and their musical tones from one day to the next. Grabmayr's sheets breathe this tension, which was obviously shared between the painter and the members of the State Opera Ballet. His work at the Vienna State Opera is about finding a pictorial equivalent for these best possible executions of a movement of the human body. In these paintings, dance and fine art come together like two siblings.

Is there anything comparable in art history? The first answer is: very little, almost nothing. With regard to art history as a whole, which is 4,000 or 30,000 years old, we should add that opera and ballet are relatively young art forms in our current understanding, less than three hundred years old. Opera and ballet furthermore were the most popular artistic medium of the nineteenth century overall, but in terms of institutional history they were separate from painting and sculpture, which formed their own academic field. This divide was further widened by the designation "fine arts" for painting and sculpture on the one hand, and "performing arts" for theater, opera, and ballet on the other.

With the beginnings of modernism around 1900, these boundaries began to dissolve. The opening of the famous exhibition of the Vienna Secession paid homage to the Beethoven sculpture by Max Klinger and to Beethoven himself, to which the *Beethoven Frieze* by Gustav Klimt

in the Secession still bears witness today. At
the opening in 1902, members of the orchestra
of the Vienna State Opera, conducted by the
then State Opera director Gustav Mahler, played
a wind version of Beethoven's *Ode to Joy* while
hidden behind this frieze. In 1917, the pro-
tagonists of modernism in Paris in the fourth
year of World War I took some pressure off
themselves by staging an opera-like ballet,
Parade, with a libretto by Jean Cocteau, music
by Erik Satie and stage design and costumes
for the dancers by Pablo Picasso.

The connection between ballet and the visual
arts subsequently continued throughout twen-
tieth-century modernism, from Dada and the
ballet *Relâche*, created in Paris in 1924 by
Francis Picabia and Marcel Duchamp, and Fernand
Léger's groundbreaking experimental film *Ballet
mécanique*, co-premiered at the Vienna Konzert-
haus in 1924, as well as Oskar Schlemmer's
Triadic Ballet at the Bauhaus from 1922, to
the interweaving of visual art and ballet by
Martha Graham, Merce Cunningham, Trisha Brown,
and others from 1930 as well as after 1960.
This in turn formed one of the prerequisites
for the fusion of the operatic form and the
visual arts in the minimal art opera *Einstein
on the Beach* by Philip Glass and Robert Wilson,
which was a major event for art, opera, ballet,
and music alike in 1976. This has resulted in
a tradition that continues to this day that is

substantially characterized by video art as a
major exhibition format.

But for a painter to spend years regularly
observing ballet dancers at close range in a
major opera house while painting pictures that
he paints only for himself, not to document
anything, not on behalf of the opera company,
but just for himself alone – when has anything
like that ever happened?

In fact, there may just be one earlier example
of such significance, namely Edgar Degas's
drawings and pastels, which were created in
the ballet school and on the stage of the
newly built State Opera in Paris in the 1870s
and 1880s.[7] Degas belonged to the circle of
Impressionists in Paris who, from 1874, had
disengaged from the art world of their time
and its ideas of painting – not unlike Franz
Grabmayr who did so from the Austrian art
scene of the 1970s. They did penance for this
with lengthy exclusion and ultimately poverty
until American and Japanese collectors arrived.
It was not until 1948 that Impressionism expe-
rienced its international breakthrough.[8] The
Impressionists sought to redefine the artistic
eye after the advent of photography, following
only their optical sensory impressions. This
constituted an artistic revolution of the
first order, one in which, among the younger
generation, Paul Cézanne, Franz Grabmayr's
great role model, played an important part.

Among the Impressionists, Edgar Degas was one of the first, like Cézanne later on, who said in view of the fleeting appearance of Impressionist paintings: we need something to hold on to, a certain stability in the forms. He achieved this in his drawings and pastel paintings during ballet exercises and at the ballet school of the Opéra Garnier in Paris, whereby the pastels he sketched hidden on the side of the stage went on to become major works of Impressionism. Degas was also an experimental photographer; his photographs of dancers, backlit and in twilight, are an example of early artistic photography. He later used them as models for drawings of dance in motion executed in the studio, which can be deduced from the traces on the photographic prints. Degas' drawings and pastel paintings from the Paris Opera anticipate Post-Impressionism from 1880 onwards and are today a prime art-historical reference. Nevertheless, they do not constitute direct painting such as in Grabmayr's work.

Grabmayr's work at the Vienna State Opera ended at the latest when Lorin Maazel took over as director in September 1982. Two years later, Grabmayr worked just as freely in the rehearsal hall of the Theater an der Wien during the preparations for the ballet *Sarapion* by Liz King, innovative choreographer and founder of the Tanztheater Wien. The artist described the resulting pencil drawings on the portfolio cover as "Körper und -teile in Bewegung" (bodies and body parts in motion). The sheets are very free and dynamic, less oriented on the specific gestures of the dancers than in the sheets from the State Opera.

The *Tanzblätter*, which Franz Grabmayr created in his studio in Karl-Marx-Hof in Vienna during the winter months from the 1980s until his death in 2015, form a large, significant and independent part of his oeuvre. Someone danced for him there almost every day during the winter months, often several dancers at once. In his own modest, yet still quite spacious rooms, he was obviously not forced to leave the location of his painting as clean as on stage or in the ballet hall of the Vienna State Opera. He was able to splatter paint as he applied it, and often splashed as much ink on the canvas or on the walls and dancers as on the sheet itself. This resulted in a yet again different level of expression.

Over a period of twenty-five years, Franz Grabmayr painted in the winter months in his Vienna studio[9], again observing the dancers for a long time and then acting in a few seconds with brush and paint, now using colored inks. These paintings on paper are abstract, non-representational in character. It is not so much the moving body that is painted here but rather the free movement of painting. This might have something to do with the fact that dances were now performed freely in front of the painter, by acquaintances, young artists, in other words by amateurs – the word is not meant in a negative sense – or by dancers from the Vienna State Opera who came to his studio, although in this case without choreography in a freely improvised manner. Grabmayr's *Tanzblätter* from the decades following his work with the State Opera Ballet form an important, yet very different group of works in his oeuvre.

What are the implications of Grabmayr's works from the Vienna State Opera in terms of art history? They come from a time when painting was on a quest to rediscover itself. The 1970s, the decade of Conceptual Art and Minimal Art, was a decade with almost no painting in the innovative contemporary art scene. In this decade, Grabmayr's double retreat, to the then dilapidated Schloss Rosenau in the Waldviertel and at the Vienna State Opera, became a laboratory for what would deliver a new footing for painting. Both places were away from the public eye, which the artist had never sought in the first place. Franz Grabmayr was thus able to develop a distinct body of work that is now set to be discovered in all its facets.

[1] Ingrid Grabmayr dates this creative period from 1972 to 1982, which coincides with the terms in office of the State Opera directors, including the expulsion that the artist mentions by Lorin Maazel at the end of this period (conversations with Ingrid Grabmayr, Vienna, June 2024).

[2] *Franz Grabmayr,* exh. cat. Albertina, ed. by Klaus Albrecht Schröder and Constanze Malissa, Vienna 2024.

[3] This was made possible by his wife Ingrid Grabmayr, who decided early on to use her salary as an accountant to finance their livelihood and that of their two sons to give him the freedom he needed.

[4] Already back then, his entire life was dominated by art. He categorically refused to apply for a job as a high school teacher for fine arts to overcome his constant financial problems, which would have had great prospects of success in Vienna's fourth district, where Favoritenstrasse is located.

[5] Cf. the monograph by Robert Fleck and Caro Wiesauer, *Franz Grabmayr. Feuerbilder – Tanzblätter – Materialbilder*, ed. by Robert Fleck and Caro Wiesauer, Cologne, Snoeck Verlagsgesellschaft 2017.

[6] These were the rooms in a small school for children with special needs that had been relocated to a school building, and which, unsuitable as a residential dwelling, had been left vacant.

[7] Cf. *The collected works of Paul Valéry* (1937), *Vol. 12: Degas, Manet Morisot*, transl. by David Paul, London 1960. The painter and the writer knew each other well until Degas's death in 1917. *Degas, Danse, Dessin. A Tribute to Degas with Paul Valéry*, exh. cat., Musée d'Orsay, Paris 2017.

[8] The Venice Biennale in 1948, the first after World War II, played a key role in this. Until then, French museums had even refused to accept donations of Impressionist works. The French Impressionist paintings on display today at the Musée d'Orsay are largely confiscations from the Japanese Matsukata Collection, with the remaining part on display at the National Museum of Western Art in Tokyo.

[9] Franz West grew up only a few yards away and had a studio in the same building complex until 1985.

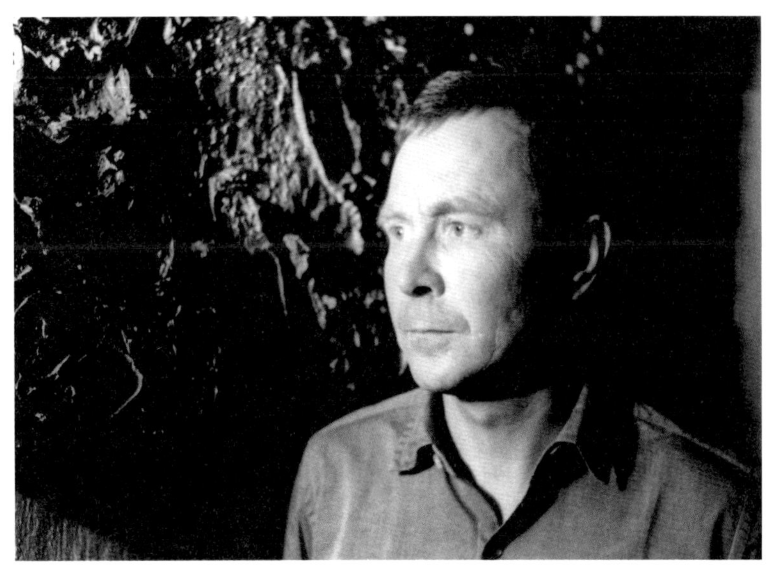

"I danced, he painted!"
Recollections by Michael Birkmeyer

"Whether I had any objections if he pursued his artistic work here in the ballet hall, he asked me," recalls Michael Birkmeyer, who was Principal Solo Dancer at the Vienna State Opera during his international career from 1972 to 1988, of his first encounter with Franz Grabmayr. "When I replied that I was probably not the right person to talk to about this, he simply said that he would rather ask those people who might potentially be hindered by his work – a polite gesture that reflected his pleasant, amiable character only too well." For Birkmeyer, this was a wonderfully refreshing departure from the norm in the artistic world: "He didn't have this over-bearing artist's manner – on the contrary, he was actually overly modest. And I liked that. Because if there's one thing I've learned, it's that people who show humility in what they do often tend to be quite talented."

In the end, it was agreed that Grabmayr's artistic activities would take place in silence. "I merely said that I needed to at least be able to hear the music, which he thought was rather amusing," laughs Birkmeyer. "So, by mutual agreement, I danced around and he, barely noticeably, painted." Birkmeyer did, though, from time to time notice Grab-

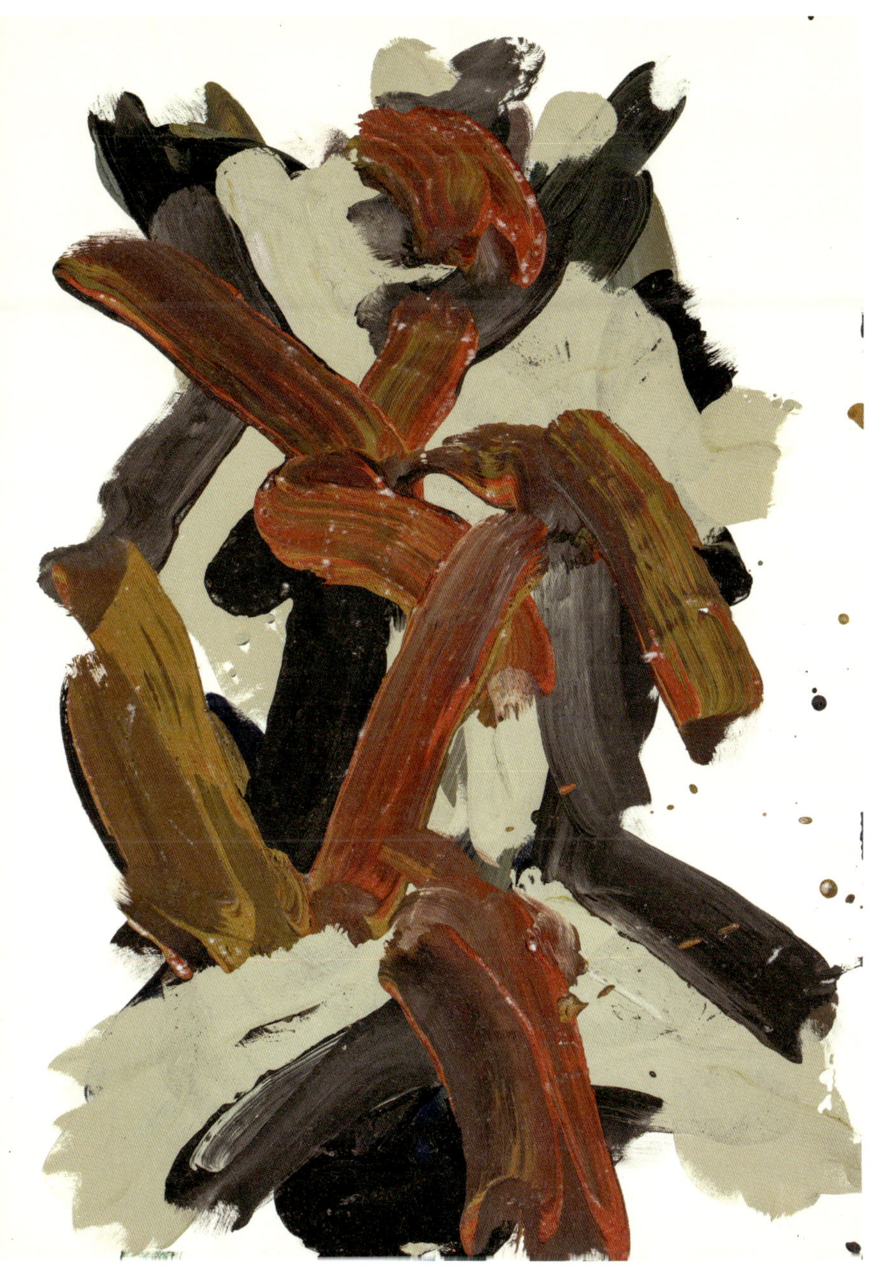

mayr's scrutinizing gaze. "He spent a long time observing before he began drawing," he recalls. "When he drew the first line, it seemed as if he found redemption at that very moment. This lightness that fulfilled him is probably what I remember most about him and his work."

In return for the "permission to paint" in the ballet hall, Birkmeyer asked for regular opportunities to take a look at Grabmayr's work: "He was delighted to show me his paintings! They had all succeeded in capturing this supposed effortlessness of dance – and they did so with the almost fairylike lightness that I feel characterizes his work." It comes as no surprise that Birkmeyer was always enthusiastic about what he saw – "I really very much liked his works". Yet he wouldn't judge whether they were any good or not: "I don't know enough about painting to do that. Personally, art – regardless of its origin – has to touch me in the sense of entertainment. And Grabmayr's work certainly touched me."

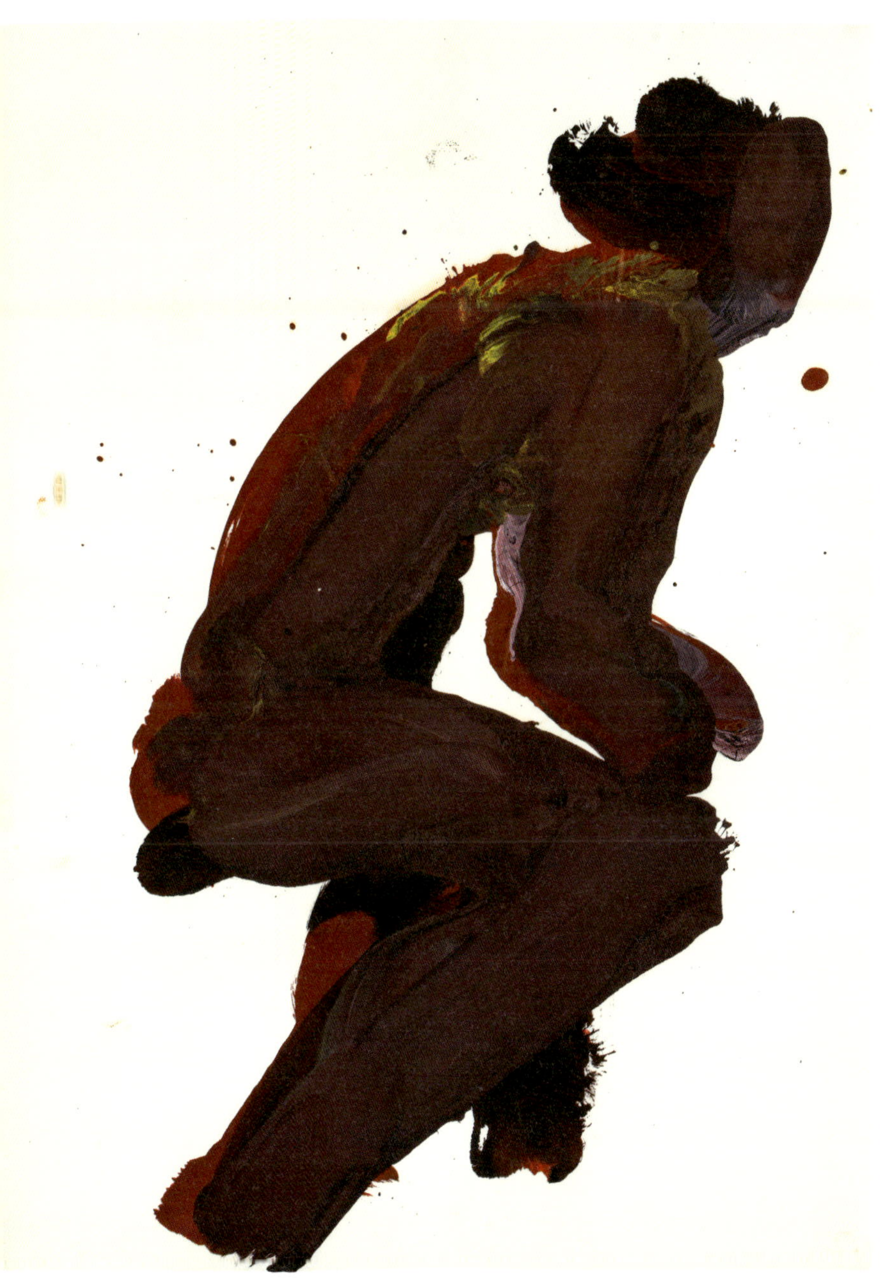

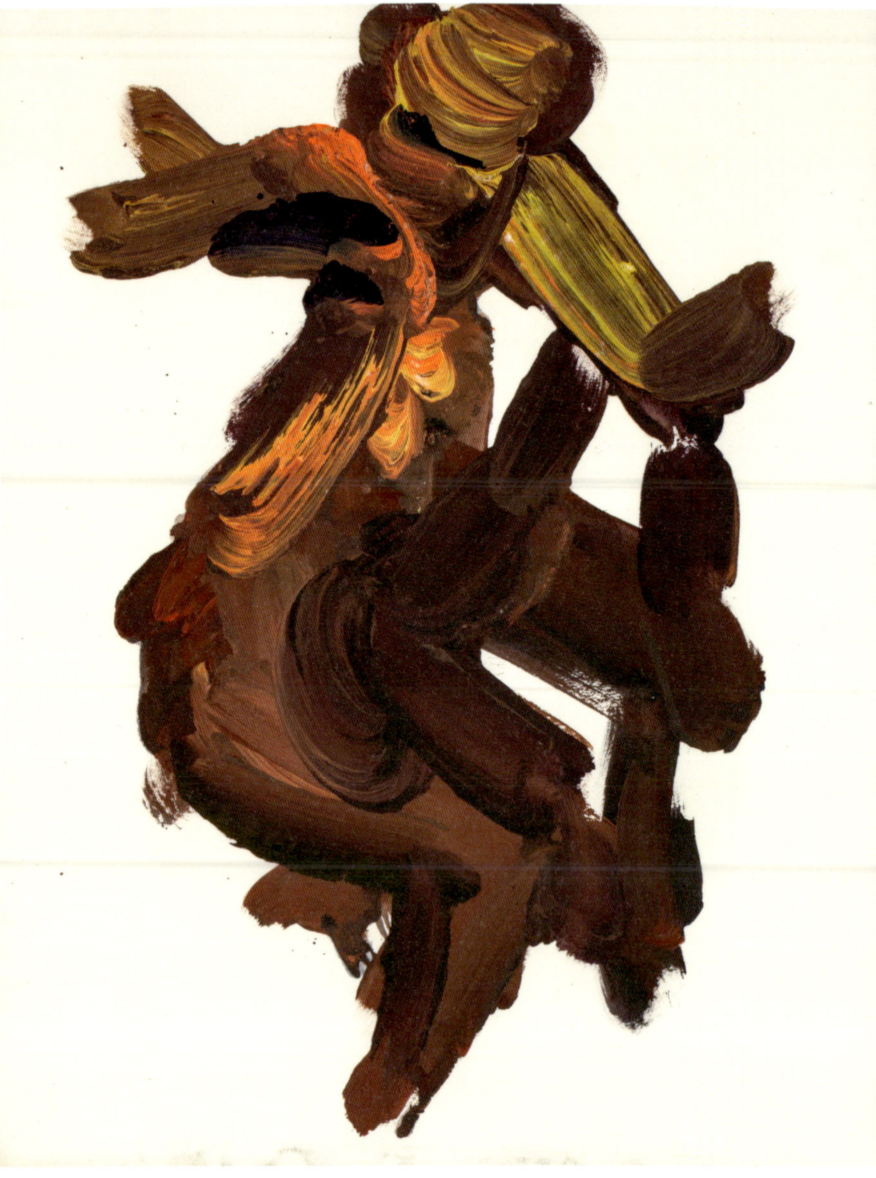

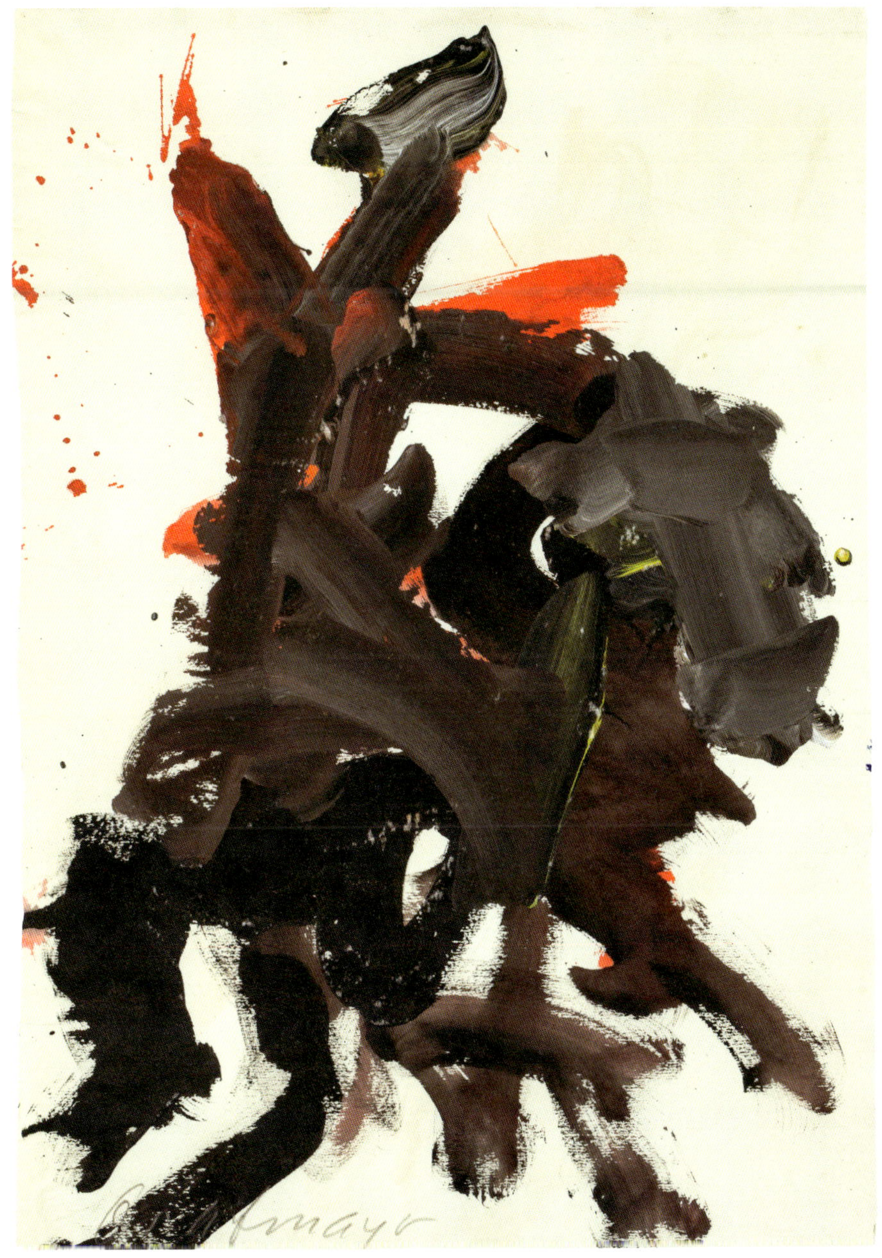

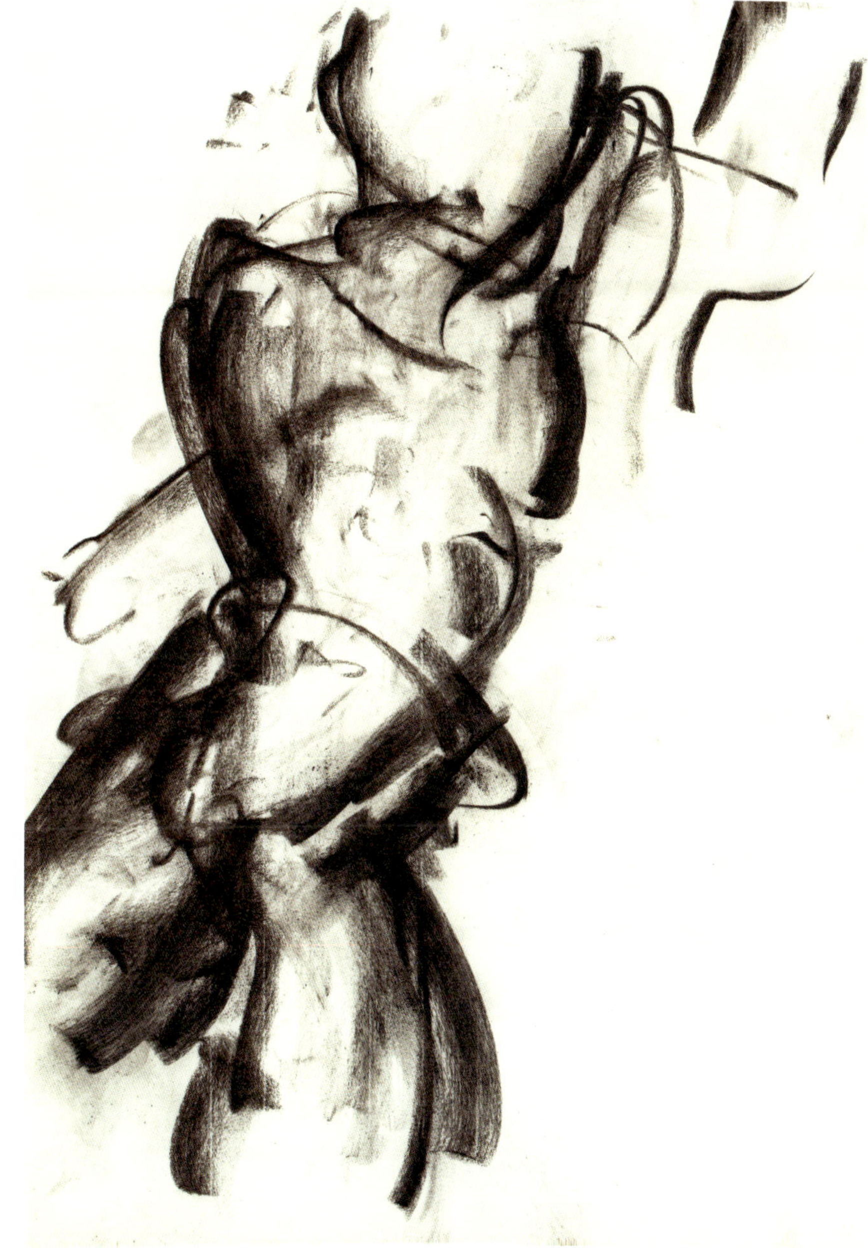

"He has never left me!"
Recollections by
Christa Himmelbauer-Ursuliak

Unlike Christa Himmelbauer-Ursuliak's colleagues, she shared a "mere" four years with Franz Grabmayr at the Vienna State Opera, where she was a member of the "Corps de Ballet" from 1963 to 1974. Four years that she will certainly keep in fond memory forever: "After all, it was a particularly exciting, extraordinary time – after all, the presence of an artist in the ballet is by no means an everyday occurrence."

It is particularly Grabmayr's "intense gaze", which scrutinized the dancers from every conceivable angle, that she still remembers in all its intensity today. It formed the basis of his work: first came meticulous observation, invariably followed by a few strokes of seemingly effortless virtuosity – his eye firmly fixed on his subject. "And before you knew it, the movement was already on the sheet in no time at all."

During this process, it was quite possible – albeit extremely rare – for the artist to get in the way of his models while observing them. "Grabmayr often knelt very closely in front of, next to, or behind me," the ballerina explains. "Especially at the beginning of his time at the opera, there were times when I felt somewhat disrupted in the dynamics of the dance. But as they say, you get used to everything," she jokes.

Besides, Grabmayr knew how to make up for the inconvenience: "One day he gave me one of his works, which showed a fragment of my dancing body from behind – that really meant a lot to me. Ever since then, he has never left me." He even accompanied her transfer to the Stuttgart Ballet, relocations to Zurich and Munich and the return to Austria in this way. "It has been fifty years that I have been carrying this sheet and thus Grabmayr along with me." A "mere" four years … as if!

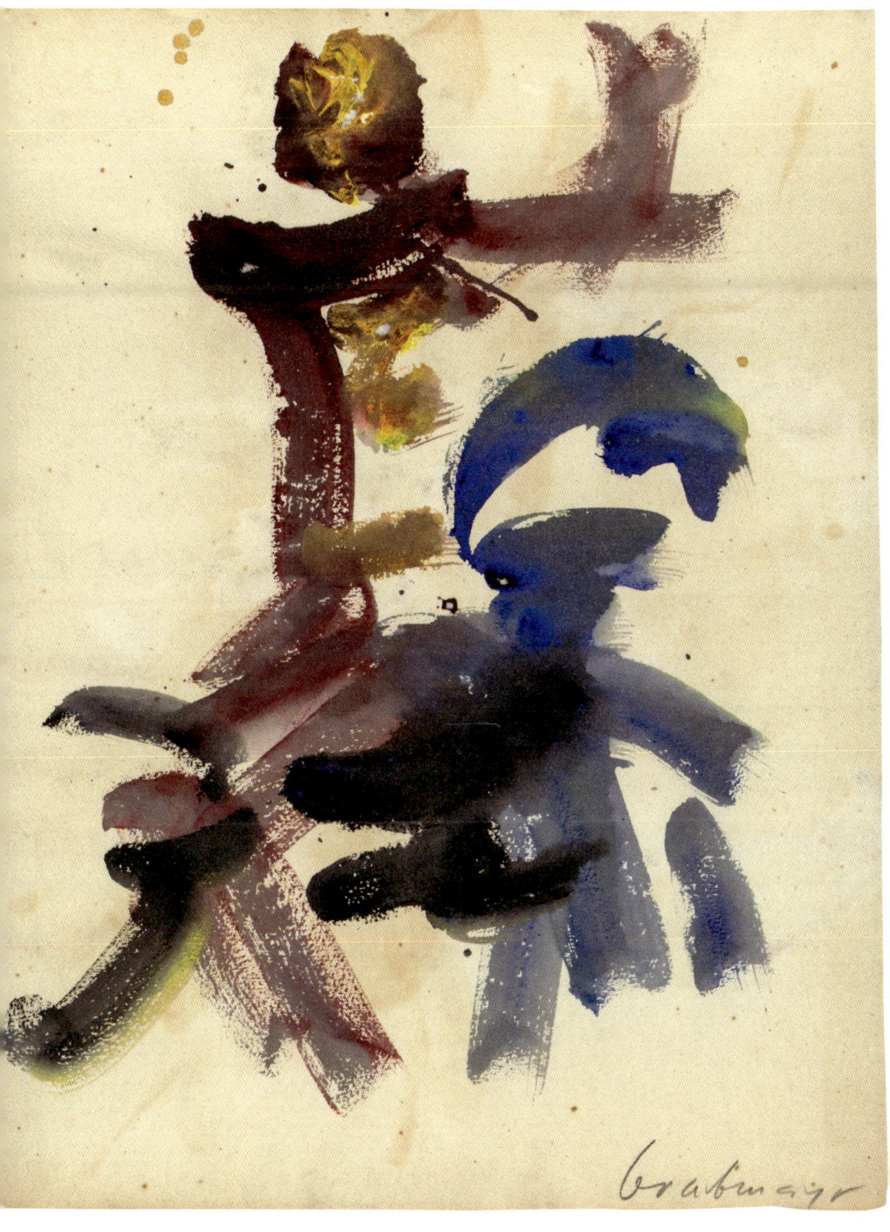
Grabmayr

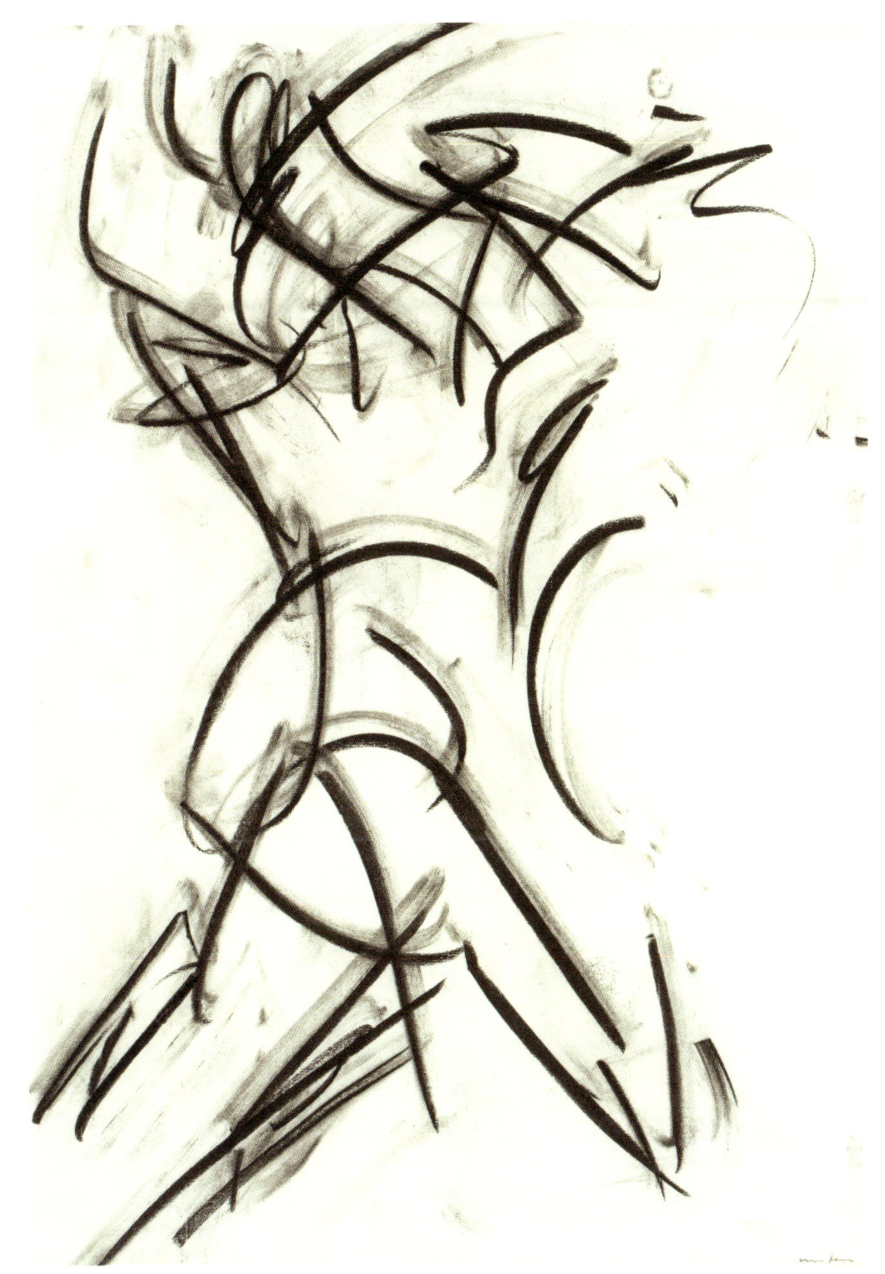

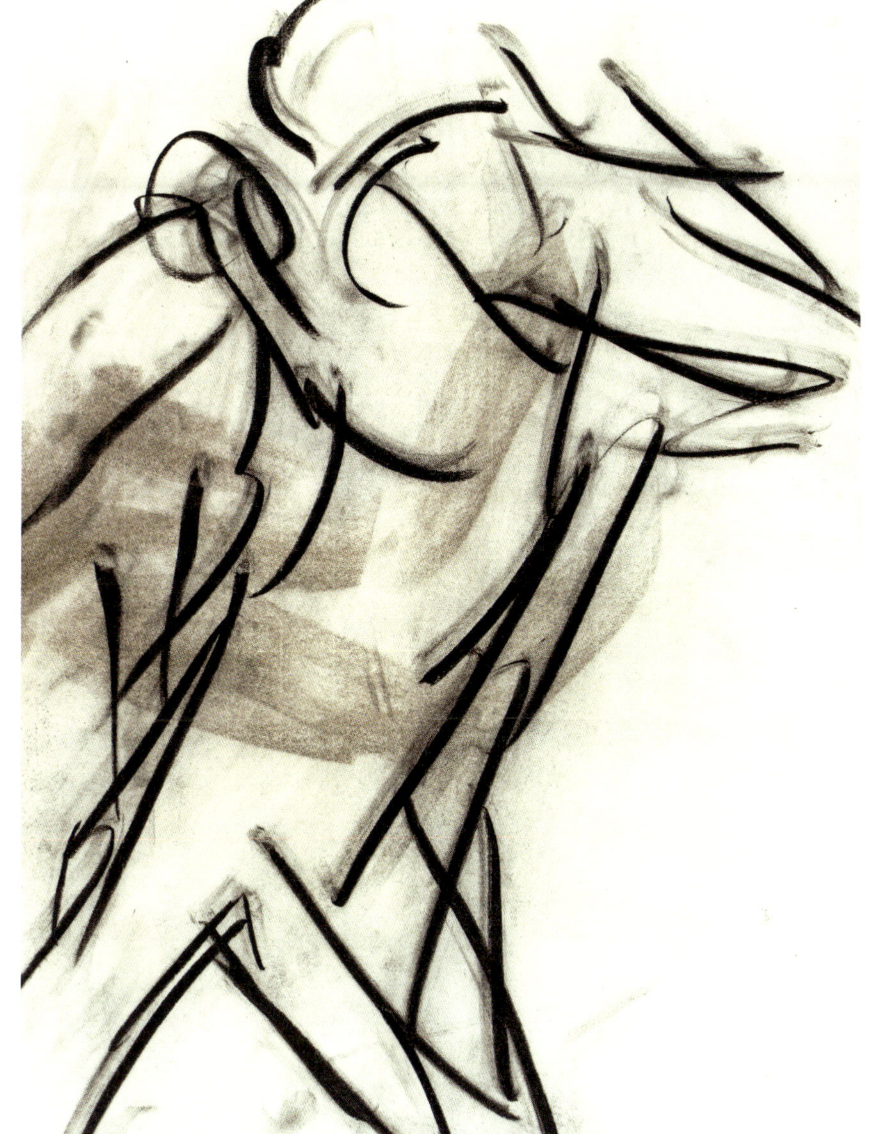

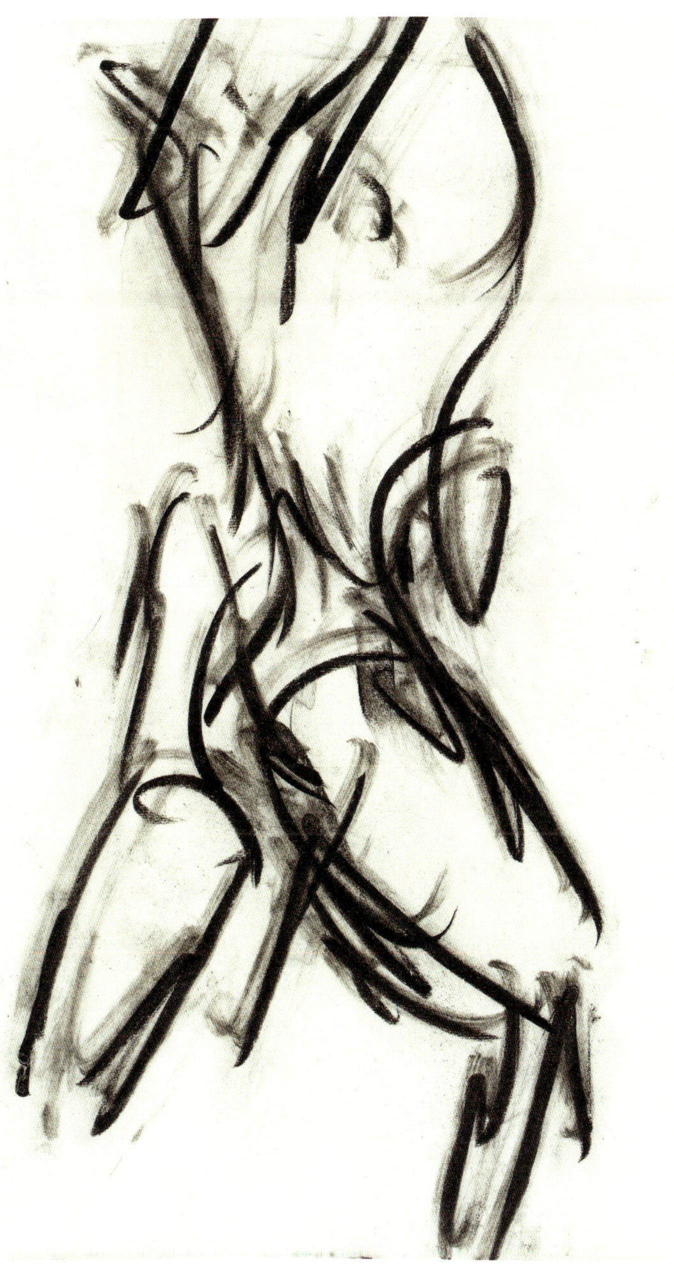

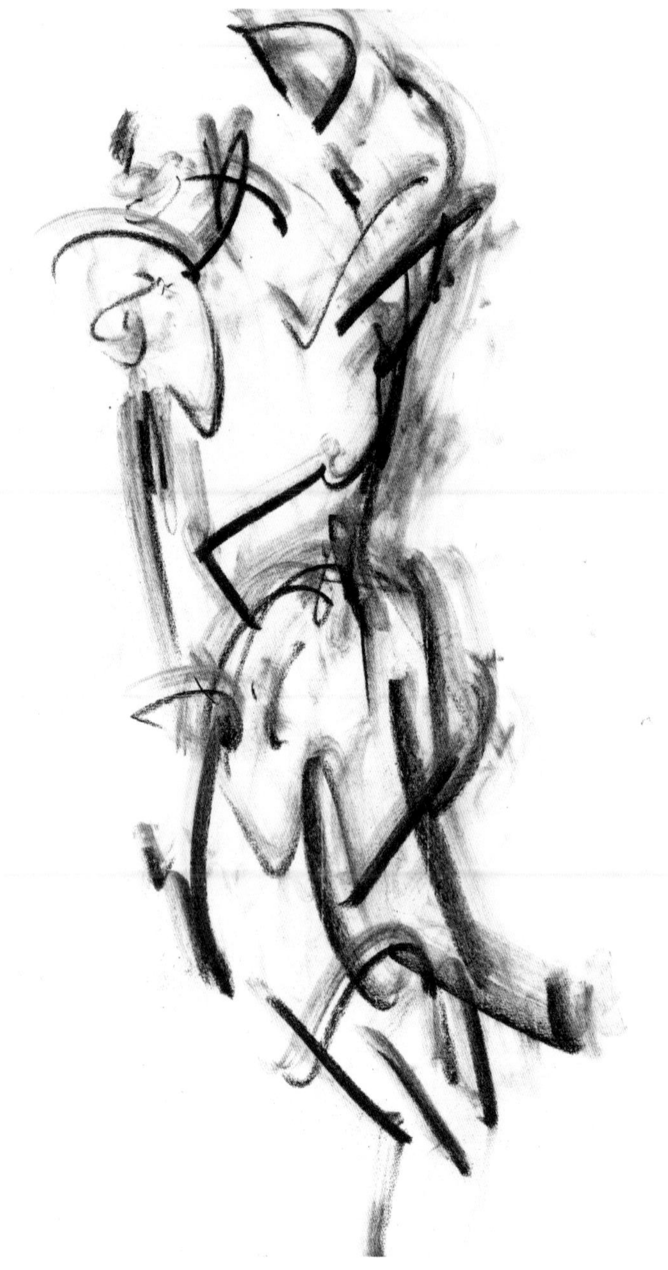

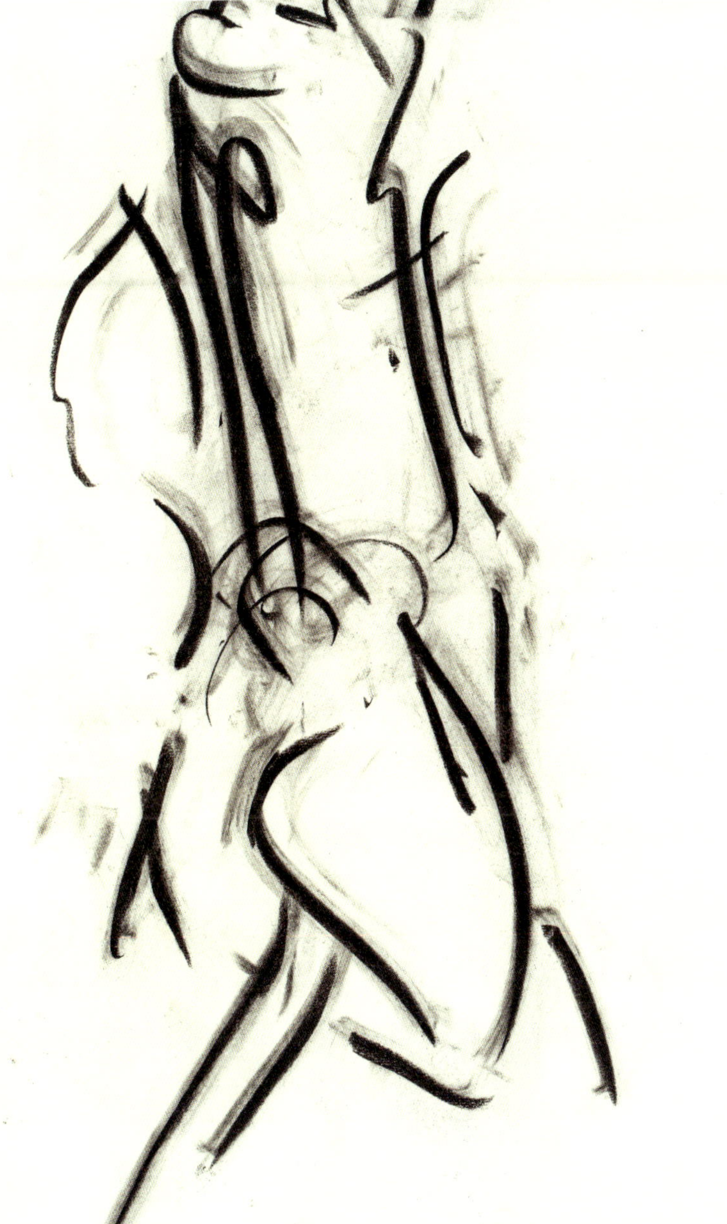

"His luck was: we liked him!"
Recollections by Susanne Kirnbauer

When Susanne Kirnbauer hears the name Grabmayr, the image of a "tall, slim man with enchanting, alert eyes and a roll of paper under his arm" immediately appears in her mind's eye. "After all, it was far from the ordinary for a Manderl (little man) in socks to sneak almost silently into the ballet hall and kneel humbly at the edge of the stage," recalls the Principal Solo Dancer, who was a member of the Vienna State Opera Ballet from 1956 to 1987. People weren't aware of the "Manderl's" activities at first: "There were no introductions back at the time – he was simply there. Nowadays that would be unthinkable."

Yet the mystery surrounding Grabmayr was not to persist for long. As soon as he spread out his paper for the first time, it was clear that he must be an artist. "He had rummaged around for a pen and immediately got to work – while his eyes were focused on us with unexpected intensity, his pen began to move like crazy across the paper." Driven by curiosity, Kirnbauer on one of the first occasions dared to look over the artist's shoulder. However, she didn't recognize herself in any of the works: "To be honest, I couldn't really make out anything – this type of painting was something completely new to me," said the enthusiastic Art

Nouveau lover. "Grabmayr had eventually tried to explain to me what his art was all about and what he wanted to express with it – as a layman, I still found it difficult to see what he was describing. But I did always like his work very much."

Grabmayr accompanied Kirnbauer's career from the sidelines, so to speak, for a whole ten years. "Keeping to himself and rather self-absorbed, he only had eyes for our movement," the dancer recalls. Looking back, it is really quite "inconceivable" that he actually worked next to the stage during performances: "This would probably not have worked without a true proponent." Who said proponent must have been no longer be reconstructed with certainty in retrospect.

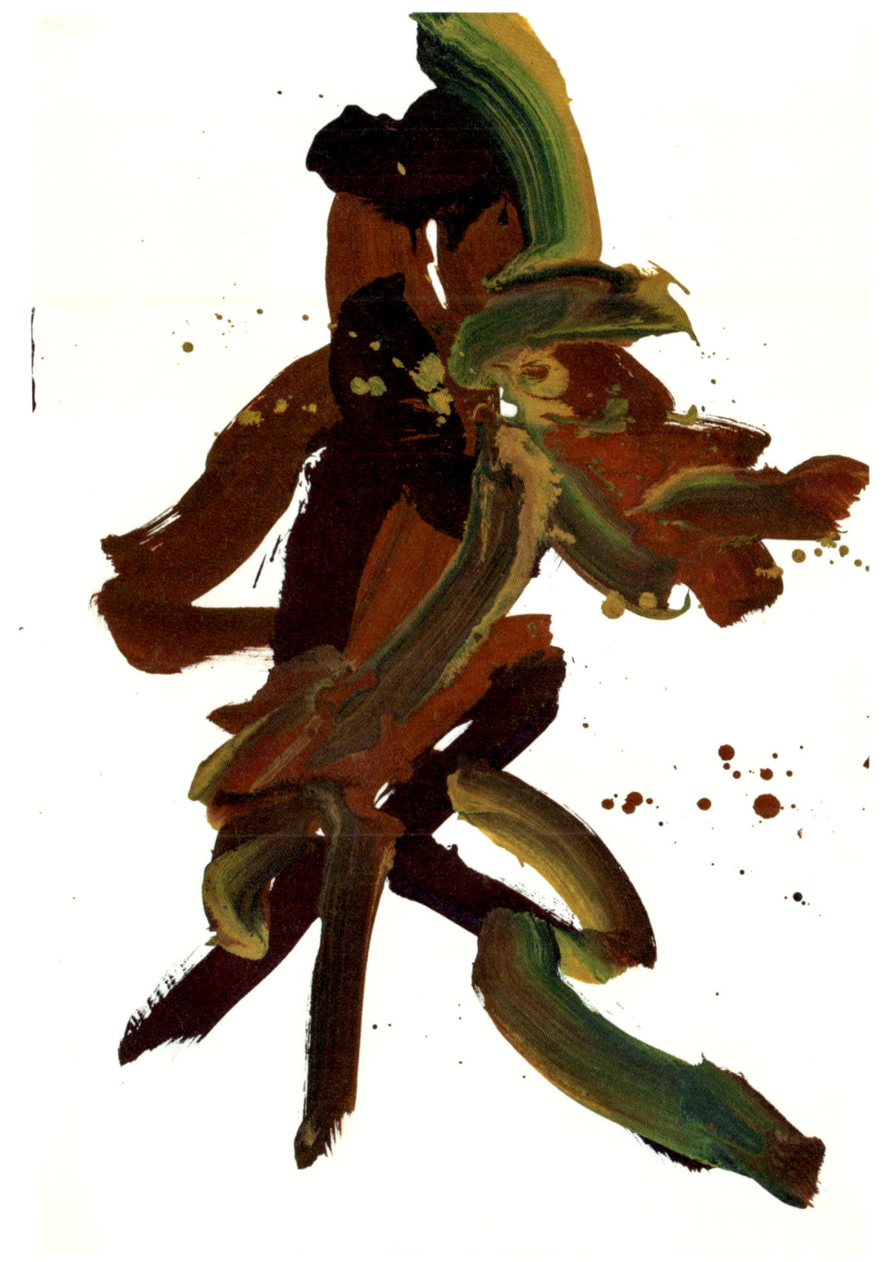

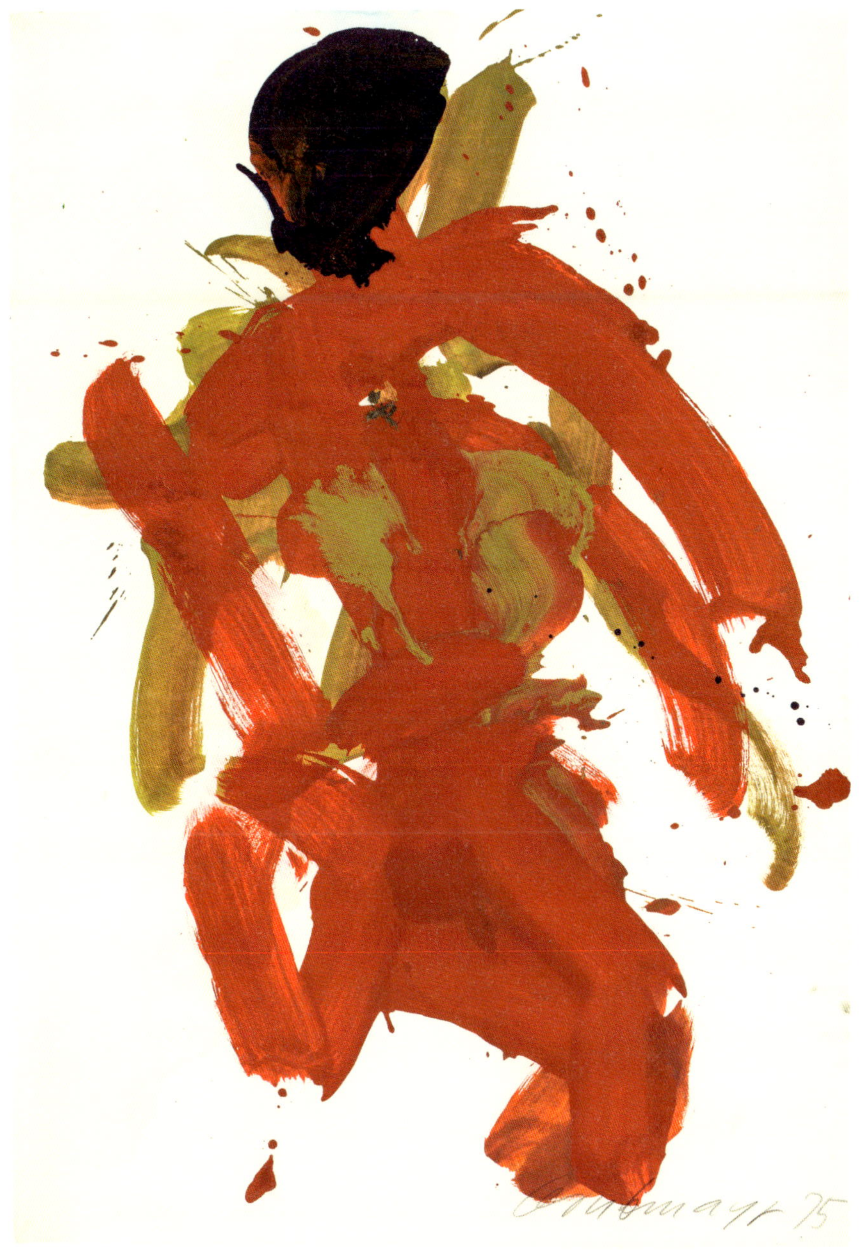

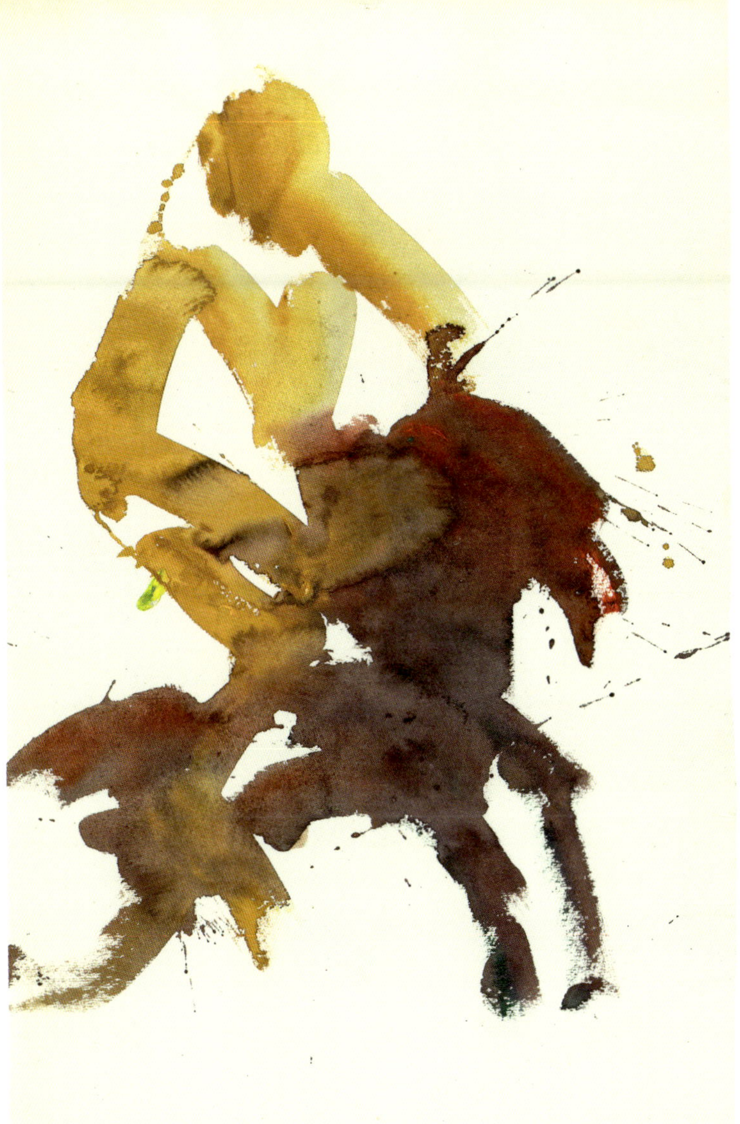

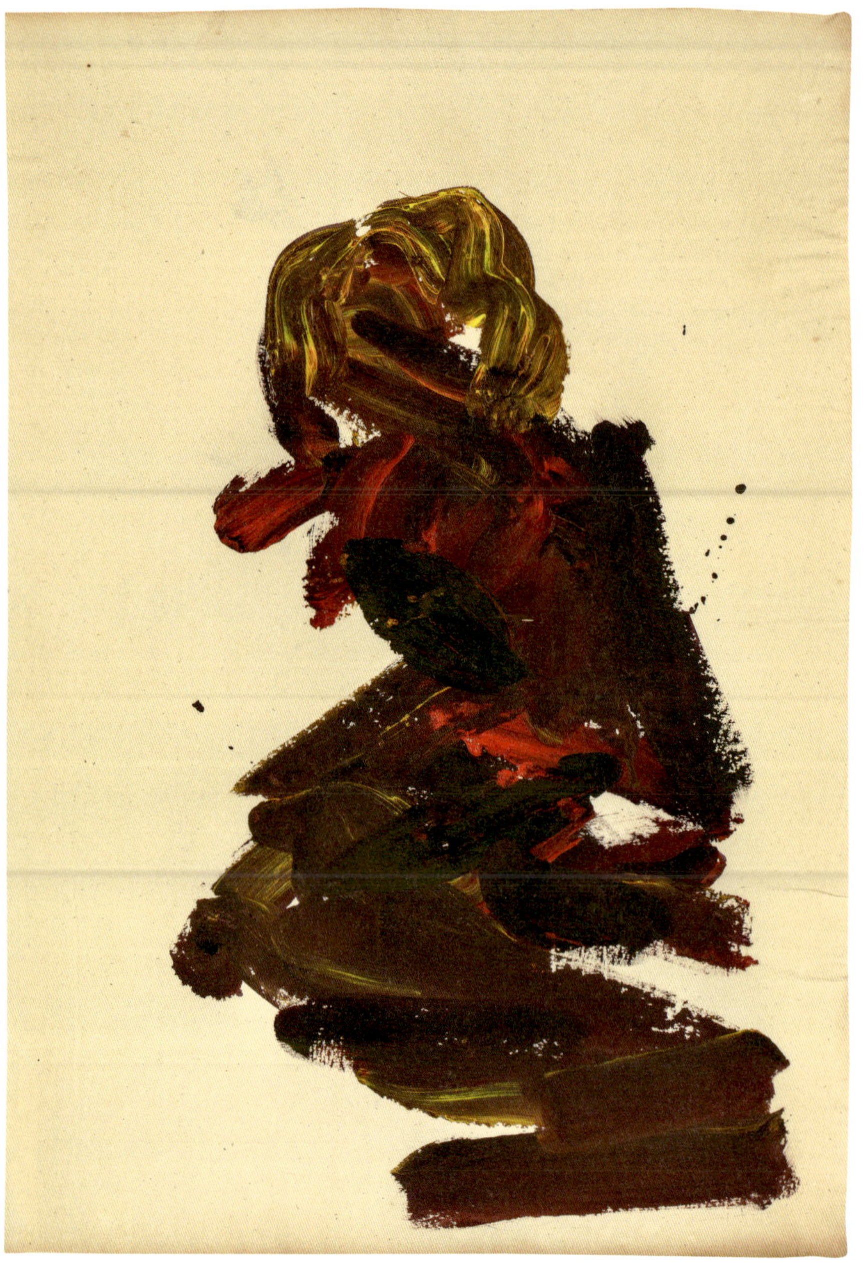

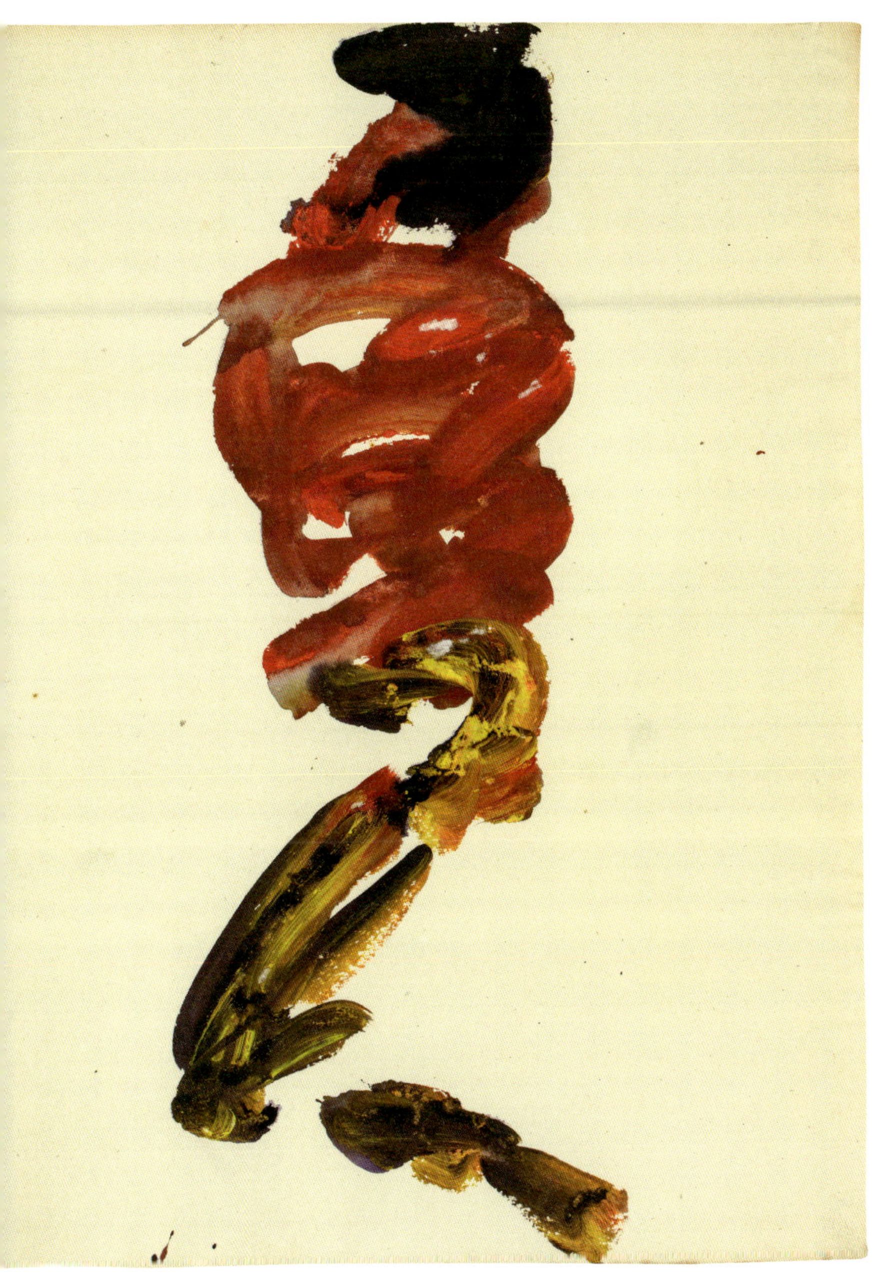

"Watch out that you don't trip over Grabmayr!"
Recollections by Renate Loucky

Renate Loucky, who was a member of the Vienna State Opera Ballet from 1957 to 1988, still vividly remembers Grabmayr's time painting at the Vienna State Opera – "as if it were yesterday," she sees him before her: "His painting and his presence were of tremendous intensity – for us he was practically part of the inventory." When she concretizes her thoughts about Grabmayr's presence, the following image comes to mind: that of a kneeling consummate artist. "We always admired him for his bent-over work," she outlines with a laugh. "We always shied away from choreographies that involved a lot of kneeling – he, on the other hand, was able to remain painting on his knees for hours on end. And all that without knee pads, which is what we would use."

He could always be found in the same place: on the right – as seen from the stage. His presence was not disruptive. At least not during rehearsals, which he spent kneeling next to the choreographers in the front row. During the performances, however, caution was required: "Because painting in the auditorium would have been unthinkable, he worked in the so-called first lane – right next to the stage exit," says Loucky. "When exiting, the spot-

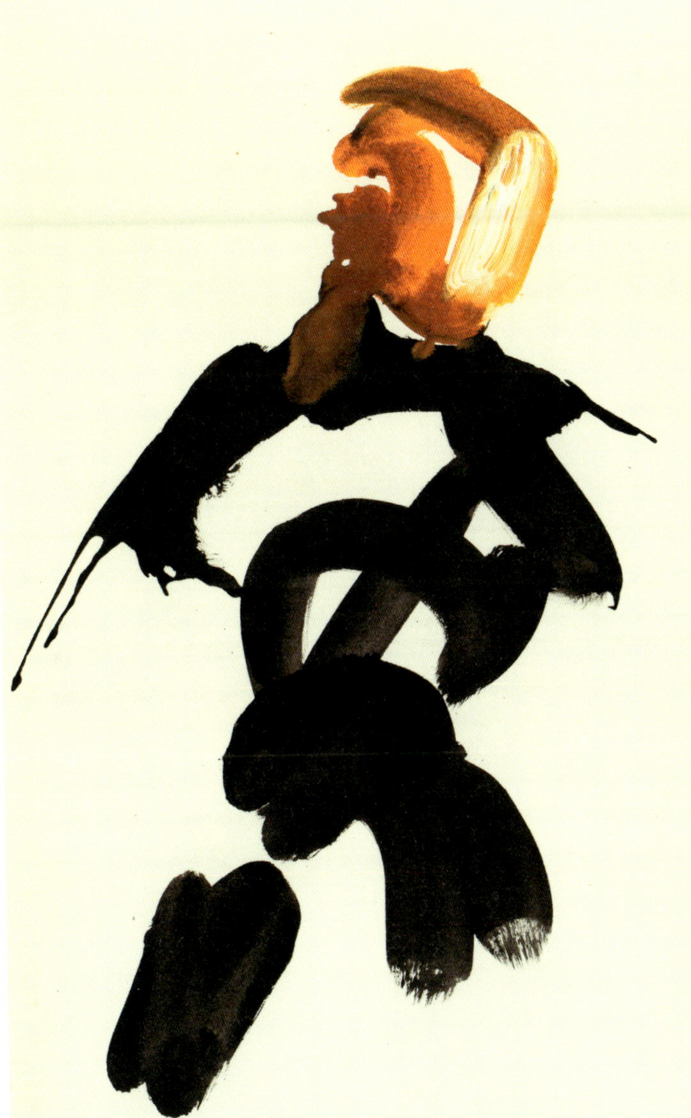

lights always blinded you anyway and blocked your view, so we often joked: watch out that you don't trip over Grabmayr!"

From his usual working spots, he scrutinized the dancers with a "fiery gaze and artistic obsession" while his charcoal pencil frantically hurried across the paper: "It almost seemed as if he was in another world during the creative process." As someone who describes her ballet career as "probably the greatest happiness of her life", she has always admired him for this fervent focus. Overall, she is a great admirer of his art: "There is hardly any stillness in ballet and yet he managed to capture the dancing figure in all its momentum."

Loucky does not recognize herself in the pictures she took back then. "That would be downright impossible," she laughs. What she does recognize, however, are the danced figures – grand jeté, grand battement and passé. At least in the earlier works. After all, the chronology of Grabmayr's graphic work is characterized by an increasing degree of abstraction.

Otherwise, Loucky's memories are mainly of a very "taciturn yet warm-hearted person" who always wore a "serene smile" on his lips: "I exchanged perhaps three words with him over the years – he was after all always completely absorbed in his art. One of those three words was 'thank you'," she muses. At the time, he

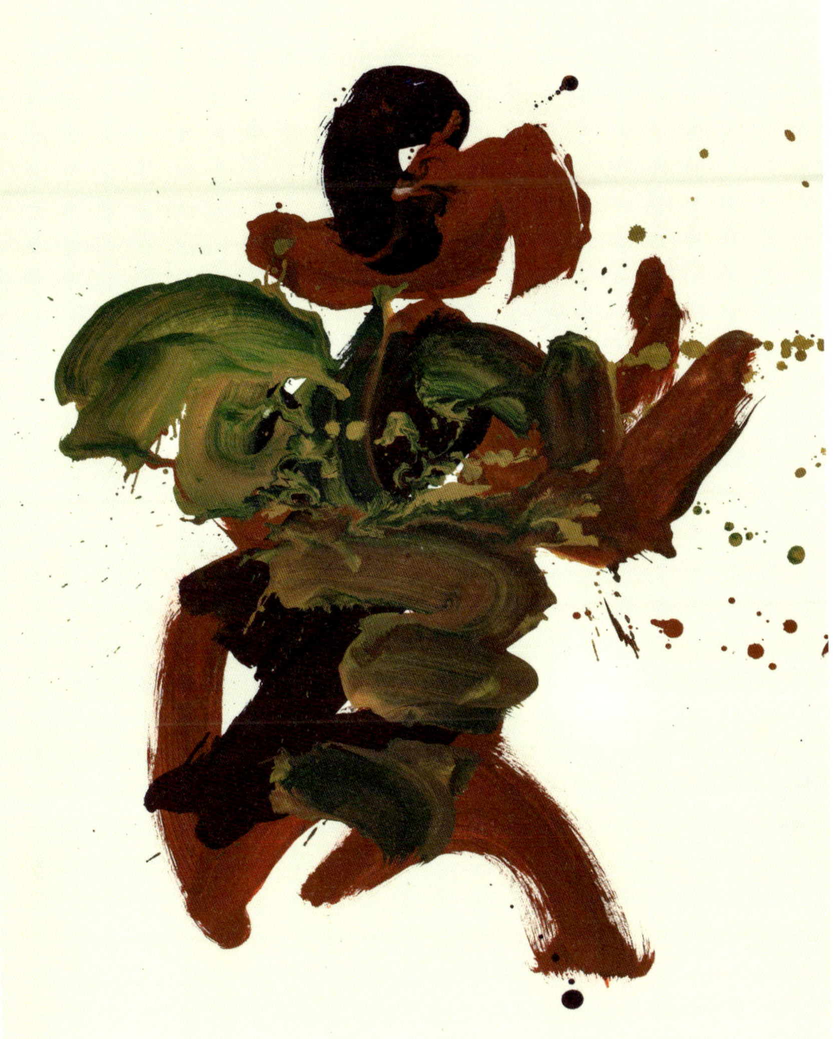

had given her one of his works as a gift – "a great sheet displaying incredible dynamism".

"Unfortunately, there was a phase in my retirement when I wanted to put an end to opera and theater altogether – that's when I gave the work to a friend who was interested in art." As fate would have it: "She later got married in the Waldviertel." And so it happened that the work found its way back to one of Grabmayr's most important places of artistic activity. Apart from the State Opera, of course.

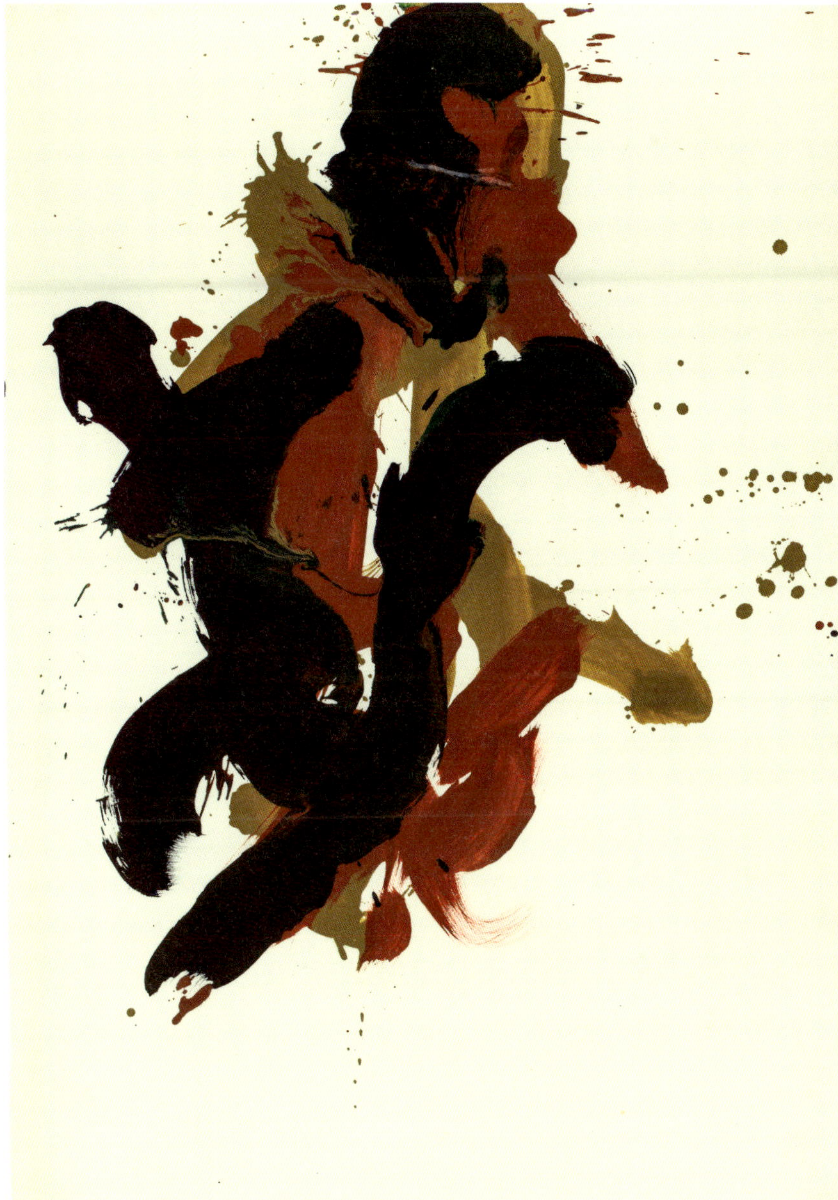

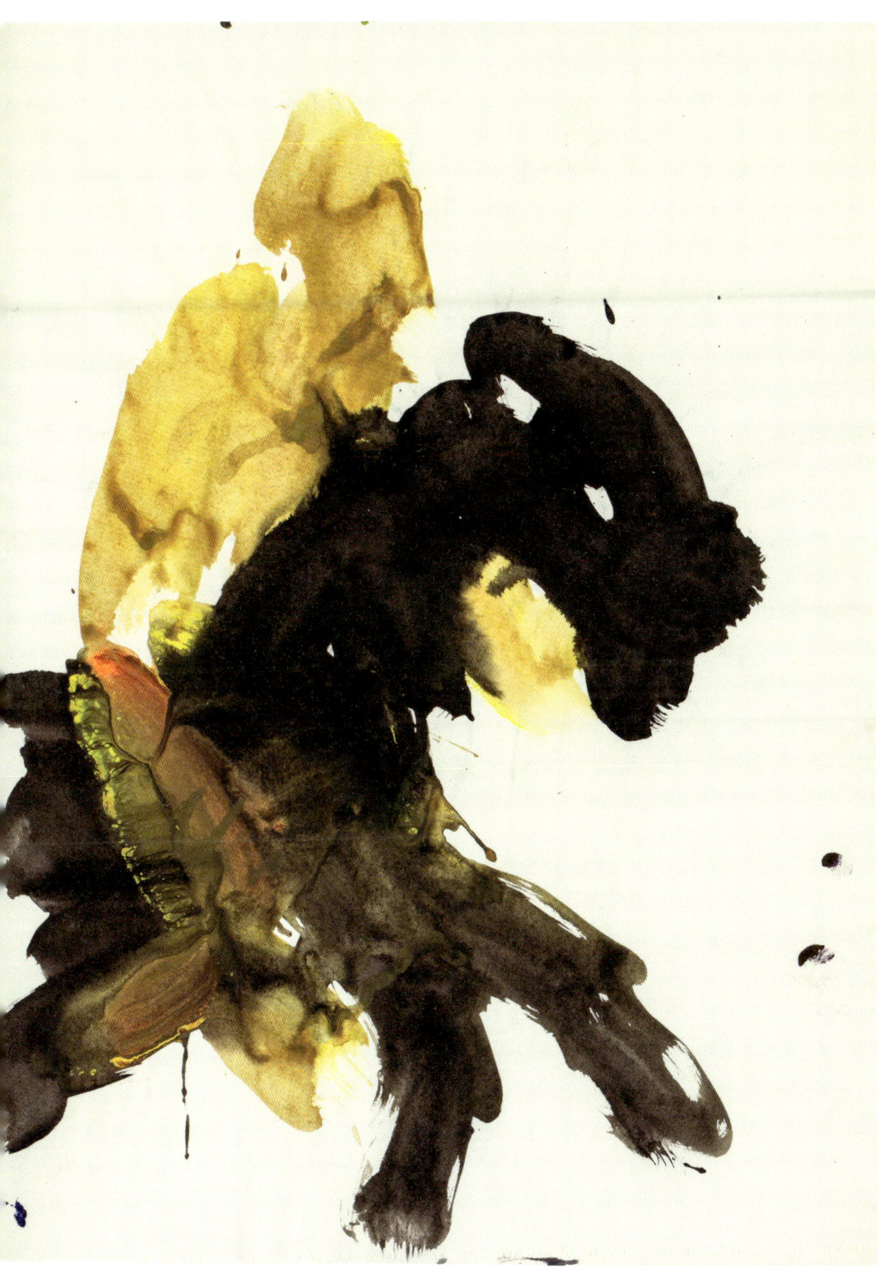

"The brush was dancing tirelessly across the sheets!"

Recollections by Claudia Androsch-Maix

It was Franz Grabmayr who made a dream come true for Claudia Androsch-Maix at the end of the 1970s. Having known him since her earliest childhood years, she was initially unaware of just how obsessed and passionate the thoroughbred artist was about art. "At first, I was simply too young to understand what a great artist Franz Grabmayr was. It was only some years later, when these gigantic oil paintings were drying in my parents' house, that I realized the true significance of his work. These oil paintings with their vast amounts of colorful paint and the richly textured impasto were incredibly fascinating to me at the time," she recalls of her parents' friend's painterly magnum opus. Her parents, Hannes and Brigitte Androsch, met Grabmayr in 1961 at an exhibition they initiated in the club rooms of the Association of Austrian Socialist Students. Enthralled by his work, they bought their first Grabmayr and from then on played probably the most important role as his first patrons at the beginning of his artistic career.

At the end of the 1970s, they told their friend, who was developing his graphic work at the State Opera at the time, about their

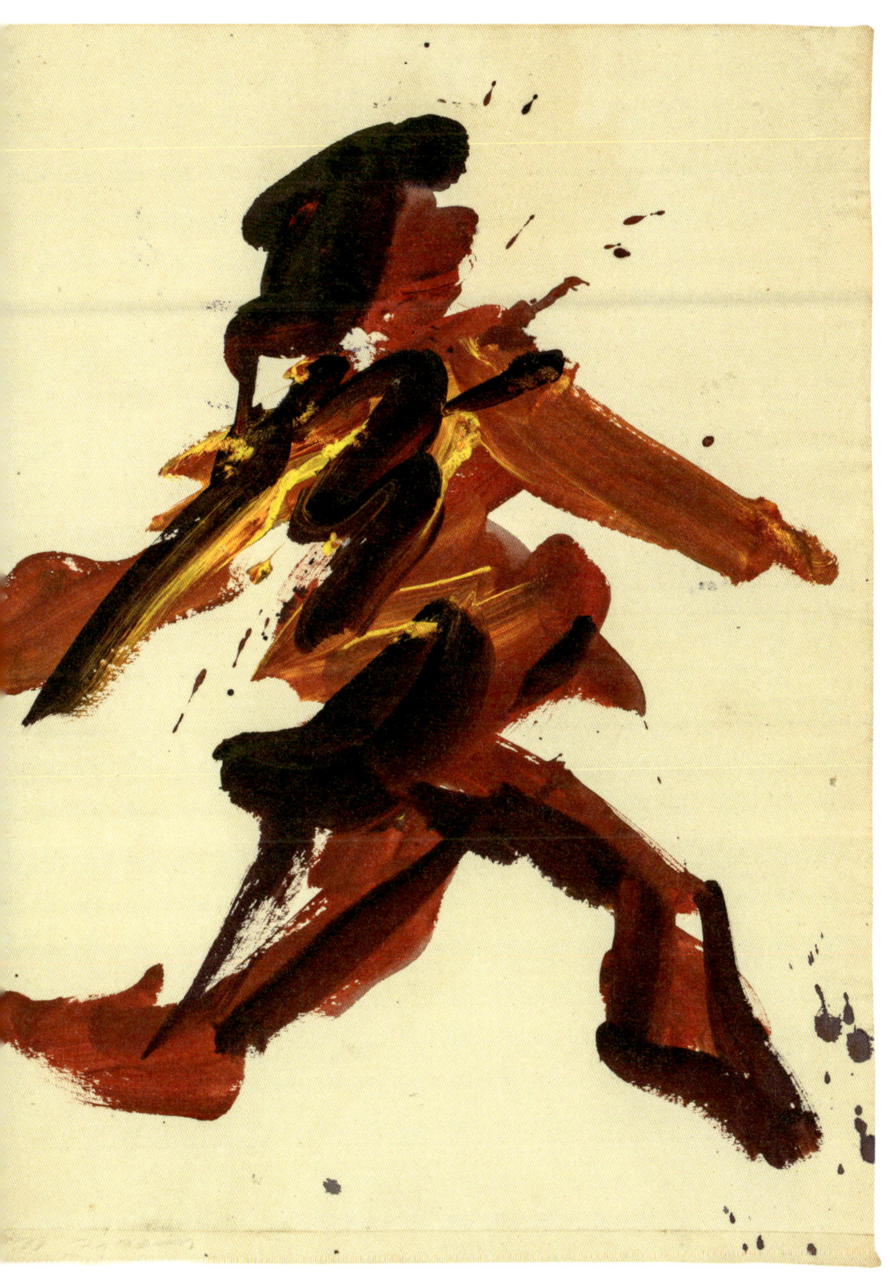

eldest daughter's recently kindled passion for
opera. And that is how it came about that
Claudia Androsch-Maix – "at the age of thir-
teen or fourteen, I don't remember exactly" –
was allowed to accompany Grabmayr's creative
process from up close: "Franz wanted to give
me the opportunity to see the workings of the
opera from the vantage point of the stage,"
she explains. "So instead of one of his private dancers who danced for him in his Vienna
studio and usually assisted him at the opera,
I was allowed to accompany him at work five or
six times." During this time, she got to know
Franz Grabmayr, whom she had previously known
as a "loving, kindhearted person", also as a
truly passionate artist. "It was impressive to
be able to watch him at work. During the first
three acts, he would always paint with ink. My
job was to take the finished, still wet paintings from the side stage alley to the back-
stage area, where they were left to dry
undisturbed and without getting in anyone's
way. After that, my work would be done – during the last act, he always switched to charcoal. The ink probably wouldn't have dried by
the end of the performance."

It was only years later that she realized
what a privilege it had been to be able to
stay this close to Grabmayr during his work.
"Back then, it was mainly the opera, the
music, thead dance that fascinated me – not

so much the visual arts. Once I even had the opportunity to experience a guest performance by the French choreographer Maurice Béjart and his ensemble." Great enthusiasm for dance – that is what she shared with Grabmayr. "With his eyes always focused on the dancers, he captured the dynamics and emotion of dance with quite an obsessive passion – the brush tirelessly danced across the sheets. It was often difficult to keep up."

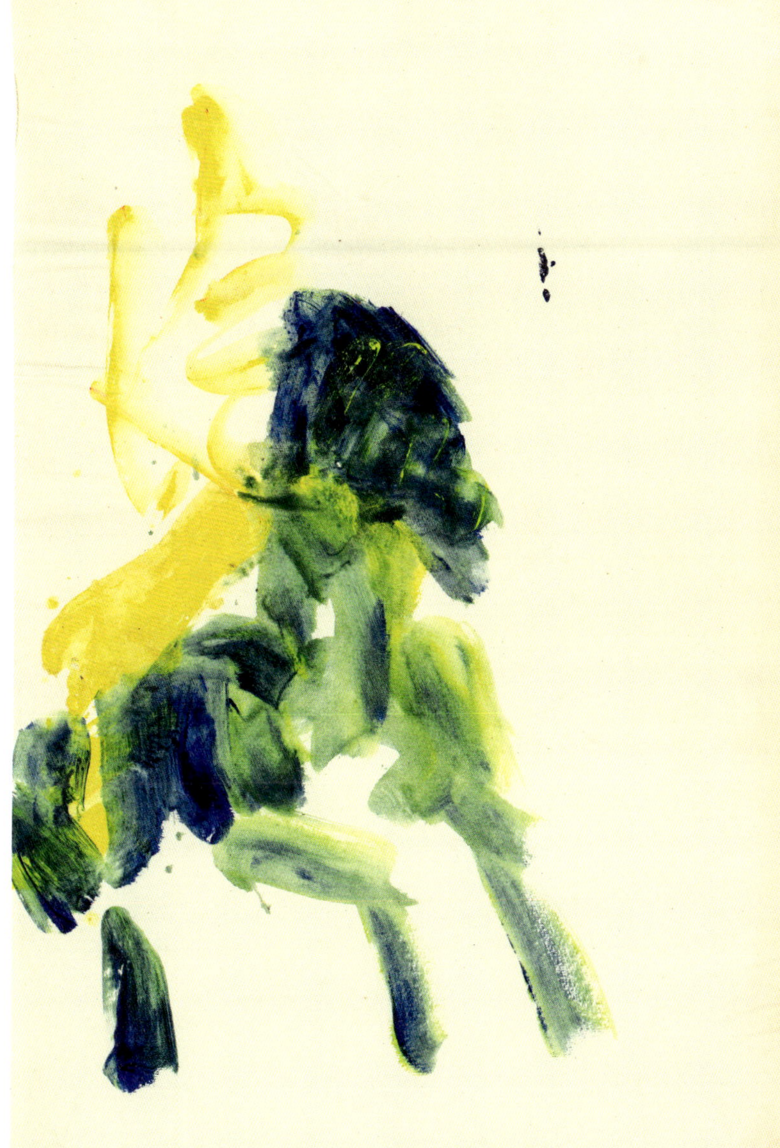

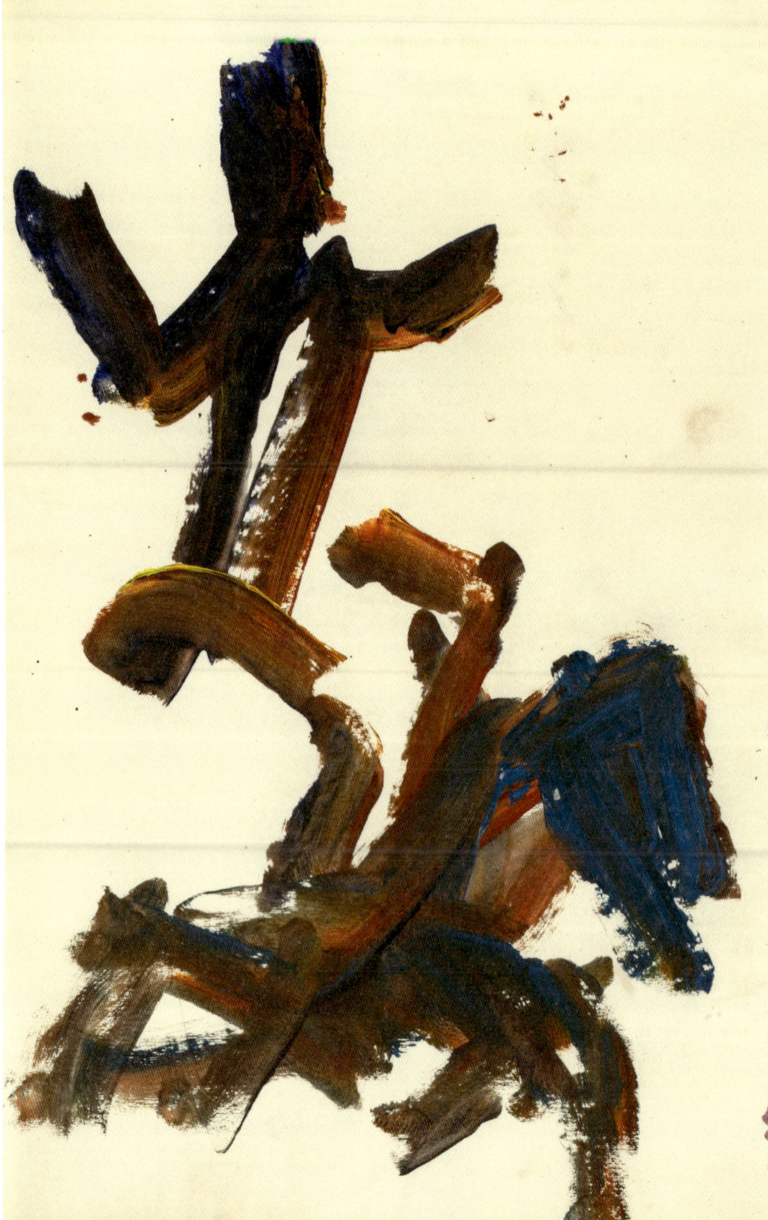

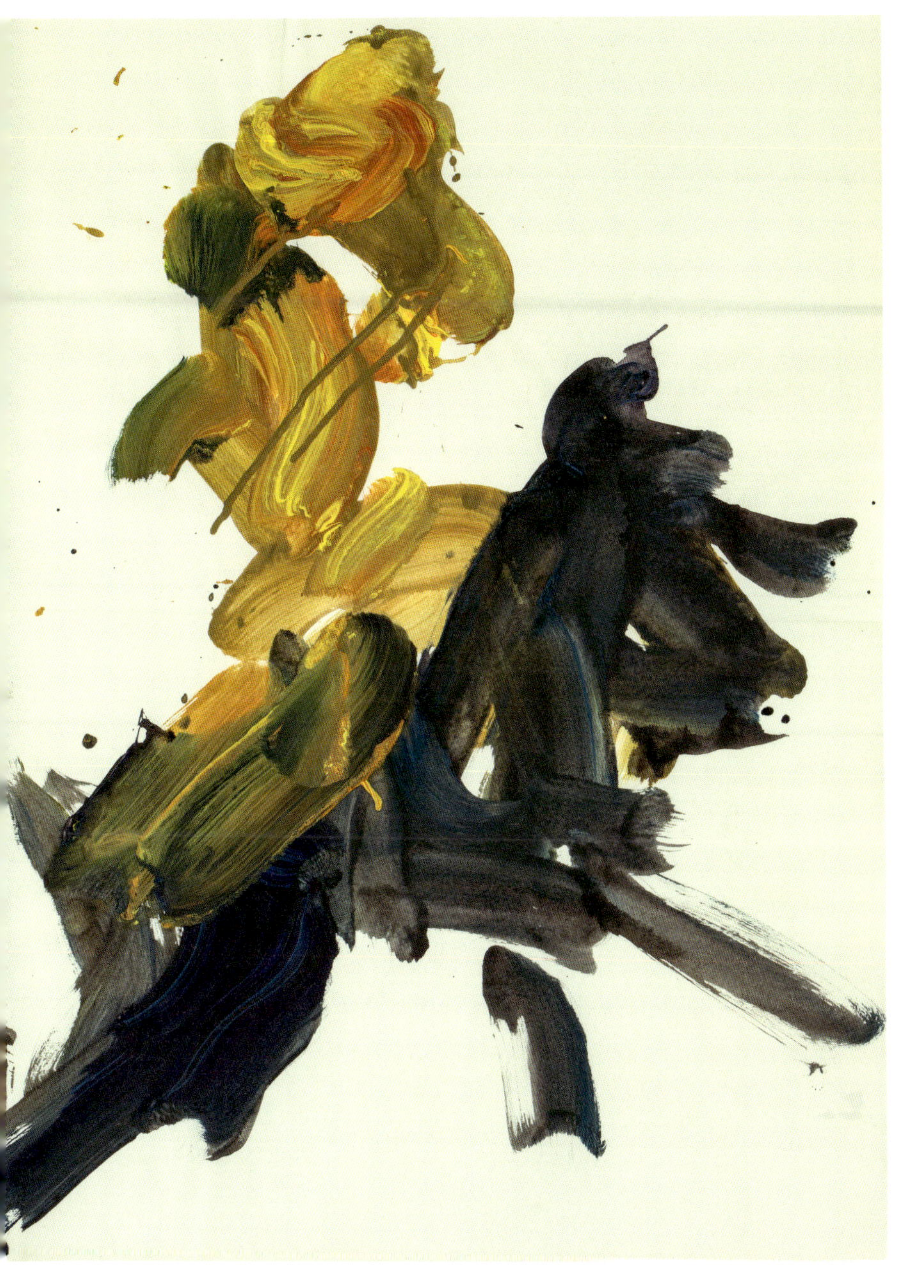

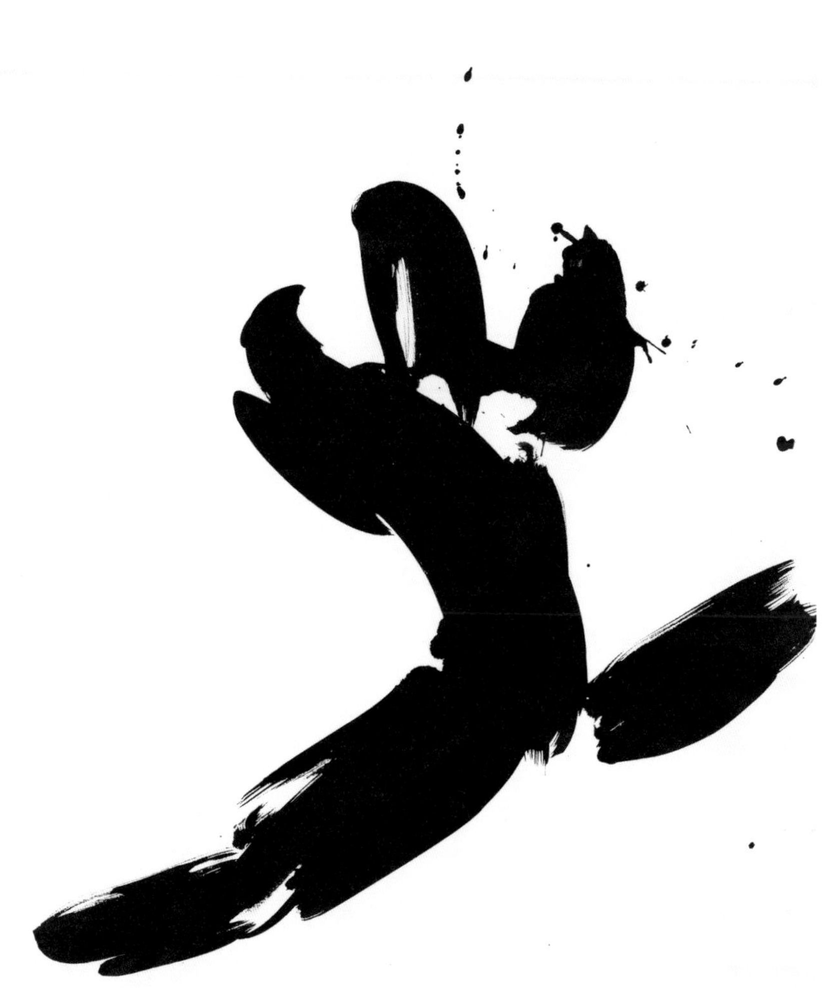

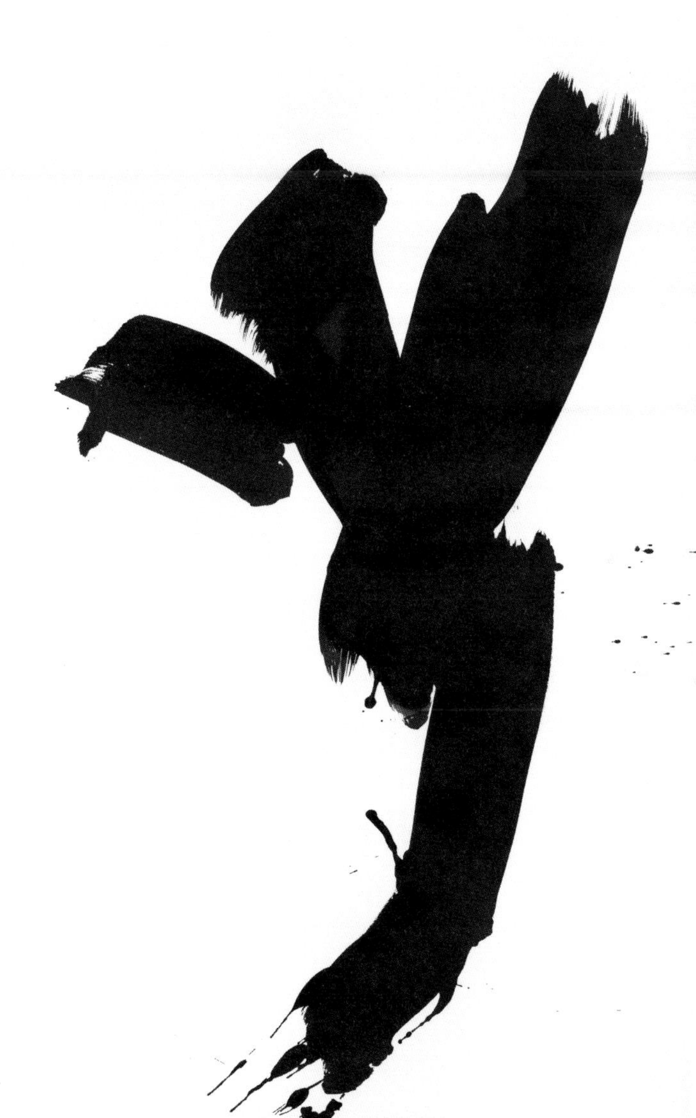

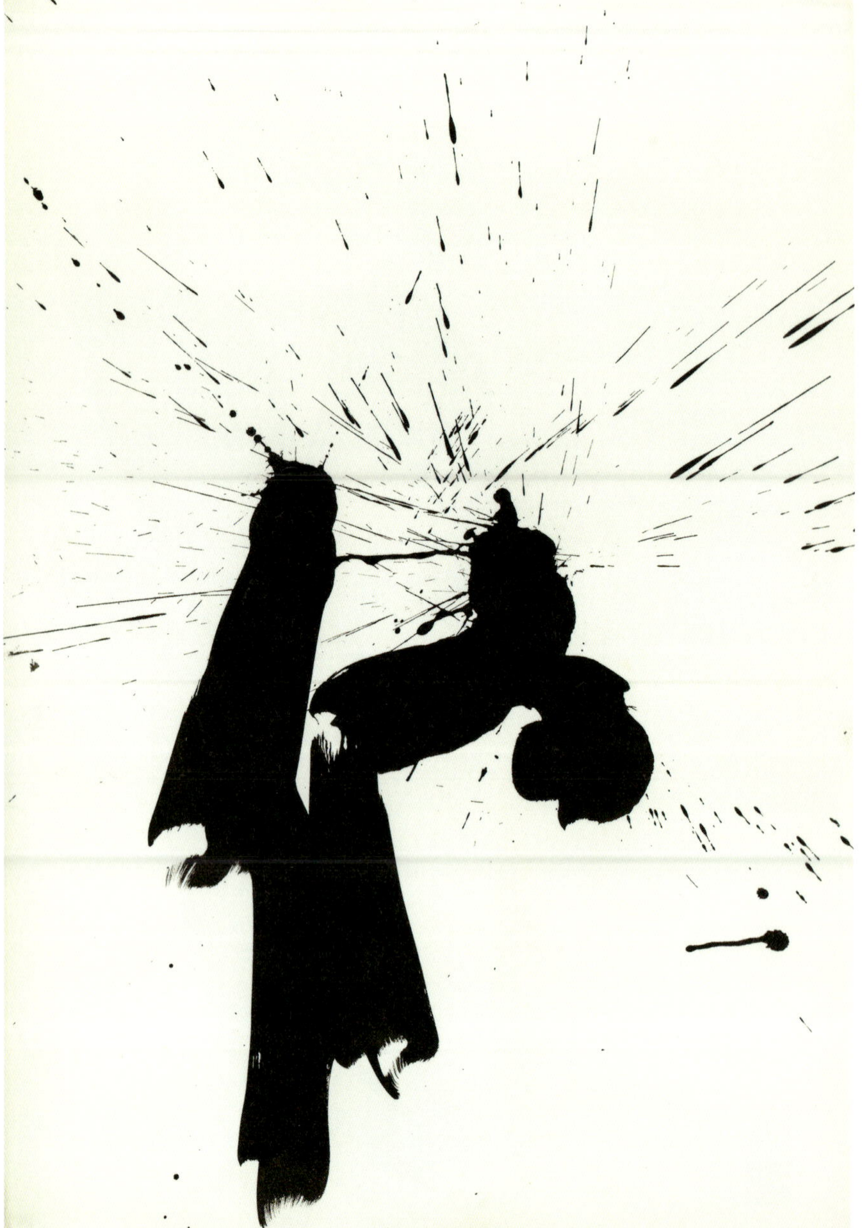

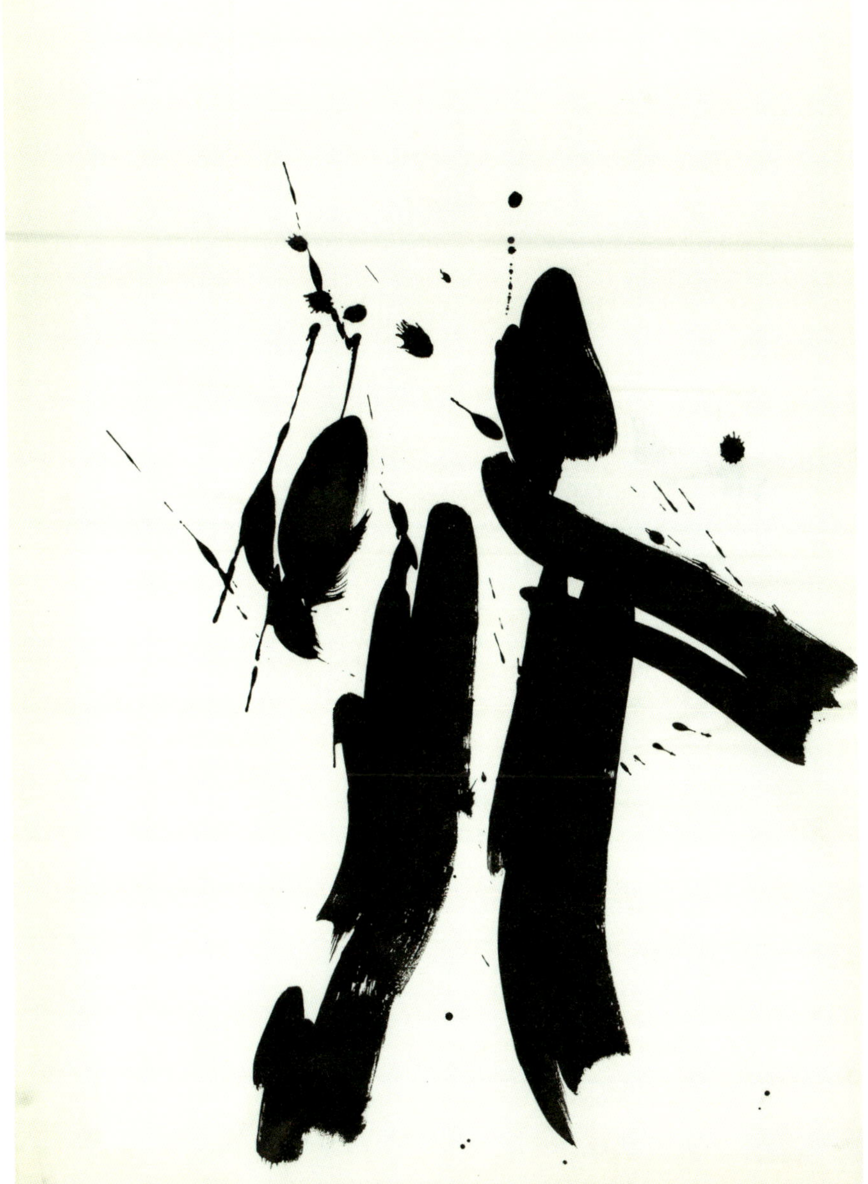

This book is published on the occasion of
the exhibition "Franz Grabmayr. Paintings
from the Vienna State Opera"
4 September 2024 – 30 January 2025
Vienna State Opera
Curator: Robert Fleck

Edited by Jakob Grabmayr / Grabmayr Estate
with a text by Robert Fleck
and interviews by Patrick Schuster with
Claudia Androsch-Maix, Michael Birkmeyer,
Christa Himmelbauer-Ursuliak, Susanne Kirnbauer,
and Renate Louky

© 2024 VG Bild-Kunst, Bonn
for the images of Franz Grabmayr and the
photographs of the works by Jürgen Seidel
Authors & Snoeck Verlagsgesellschaft, Cologne

Production
Snoeck Verlagsgesellschaft, Nievenheimer Str. 18,
50739 Cologne: www.snoeck.de

Photography: Jürgen Seidel, Bonn
Lithography: Erik Heckens, Grieth
Translation: Susie Hondl

ISBN 978-3-86442-448-9
Printed in Germany

Special thanks to Bogdan Roscic, Director of the
Vienna State Opera, who has supported and welcomed
this exhibition project from the very beginning.

Media partner of the Grabmayr Estate:
VGN Medien Holding, Wien

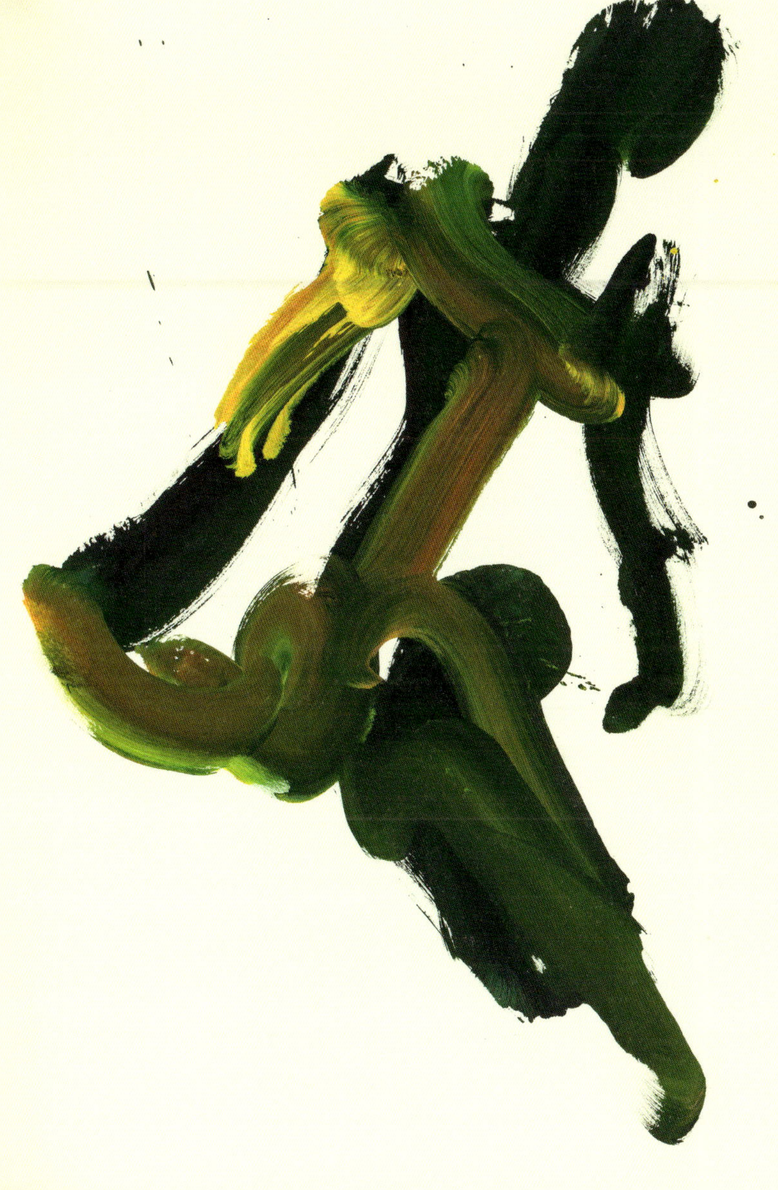